Contents

BARBARA L. BROCK   MARILYN L. GRADY

Developing a Teacher Induction Plan

A Guide for School Leaders

CORWIN PRESS
A SAGE Publications Company
Thousand Oaks, California

For information:

Corwin Press
A Sage Publications Company
2455 Teller Road
Thousand Oaks, California 91320
www.corwinpress.com

Sage Publications Ltd.
1 Oliver's Yard
55 City Road
London EC1Y 1SP
United Kingdom

Sage Publications India Pvt. Ltd.
B-42, Panchsheel Enclave
Post Box 4109
New Delhi 110 017 India

Printed in the United States of America.

Library of Congress Cataloging-in-Publication Data

Brock, Barbara L.
Developing a teacher induction plan : a guide for
school leaders / Barbara L. Brock, Marilyn L. Grady.
      p. cm.
Includes bibliographical references and index.
ISBN 0-7619-3112-0 (cloth) — ISBN 0-7619-3113-9 (pbk.)
   1. First year teachers—Supervision of. I. Grady, Marilyn L. II. Title.
LB2844.1.N4B758 2006
371.2'03—dc22

                                                           2005019976

This book is printed on acid-free paper.

05   06   07   08   09   10   9   8   7   6   5   4   3   2   1

Acquisitions Editor:	Elizabeth Brenkus
Editorial Assistant:	Candice Ling & Desirée Enayati
Production Editor:	Jenn Reese
Typesetter:	C&M Digitals (P) Ltd.
Proofreader:	Jennifer Withers
Indexer:	Ellen Slavitz
Cover Designer:	Tracy Miller
Graphic Designer:	Scott Van Atta

Developing a Teacher Induction Plan

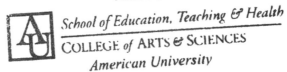

Courtesy of the
School of Education, Teaching & Health
COLLEGE *of* ARTS & SCIENCES
American University

This book is dedicated to our family cheering sections, for their consistent support:
Mike, Dave, Eric Brock, and Corinne Baker . . . B.B.
The Memphis-Graceland Team: Justin and Elizabeth Grady and Their Auntie . . . M.G.

List of Exercises

Preface

In the 1980s, school districts began to realize the importance of beginning teacher induction programs. Faced with high teacher attrition and a growing student population, many districts abandoned the "survival of the fittest" method and sought more effective means of retaining and developing promising new teachers (Brewster & Railsback, 2001; Moir, 2003; RNT, 2000).

The number of schools and school districts that have adopted teacher induction programs is growing (Moir, 2003). The scope of the programs, however, varies widely from one-day orientation programs to developmental programs lasting up to three years. Induction for roughly 50% of all beginning teachers continues to consist of an orientation program (DePaul, 2000), although some school districts provide substantial induction programs as the initial step in a continuous career-long professional development program.

The requirements of the No Child Left Behind Act have given impetus to state initiatives to improve teacher quality. A growing number of states mandate teacher induction programs for their school districts, some of which are linked with assessments necessary for license renewal and continuing employment (Ganser, 2003). The U.S. Department of Education has taken steps to improve the American teaching force through legislation aimed at improving teacher education and working with college presidents to call attention to teacher education (U.S. Department of Education, 2002).

In spite of the growing interest in teacher induction, support for it is missing or inadequate, and new teachers continue to leave the teaching field at a rate of 20% to 30% within the first three years. By the end of five years, approximately 50% of new teachers will have left the field (DePaul, 2000). Other beginning teachers, disillusioned and uninspired, remain in the field to the detriment of their students.

Clearly, teacher induction programs hold the answer to retaining and developing promising beginning teachers. The challenge is creating an effective program.

Designed with school leaders and staff developers in mind, *Developing a Teacher Induction Plan: A Guide for School Leaders* offers practical assistance for creating and implementing a teacher induction program. The first chapter is a discussion of the role of the induction team and the needs of the recipients of induction programs. Chapters 2 and 3 focus on assessment of current problems, past performance, and school context. Chapters 4 through 10 guide the reader through the process of designing an induction program to meet school needs.

The book has a workbook format—read it, discuss it, and write in it. We recommend that you and your planning team complete the chapters in order. You may be tempted to skip the opening chapters on assessment and begin with induction program design. In skipping the assessment exercises, however, you run the risk of creating an induction program based on assumptions about your school rather than an appraisal of its actual needs. Thoughtful assessment of current problems, the school context, and past practice is essential to the creation of an induction program that meets the specific needs of a school. After completing the exercises in the book, you will have developed a plan for a teacher induction program tailored to meet the needs of your school.

Barbara L. Brock

Marilyn L. Grady

Acknowledgments

We extend appreciation and thanks to the following individuals whose efforts and talents made our work possible: Cindy DeRyke and Susan McCoy, University of Nebraska-Lincoln, for their manuscript preparation expertise, and Lynn Schneiderman, Creighton University's Reinert Alumni Library, for her patient and efficient research assistance.

Corwin Press gratefully acknowledges the contributions of the following reviewers:

Jacqueline Colbert, Assistant Director
Division of School Improvement
North Carolina Department of Public Instruction
Raleigh, NC

Kenneth Goodwin, Principal
P.S. DuPont Elementary School
Wilmington, DE

Mary Johnstone, 2004 NAESP National Distinguished Principal
Susitna Elementary School
Anchorage, AK

Teresa N. Miller, Associate Professor
Department of Educational Administration
College of Education
Kansas State University
Manhattan, KS

Charlotte Tharp, Mentoring/Induction Consultant
Powerful Allies for Learning Support (PALS)
Ben Wheeler, TX

Jerry Vaughn, 2004 NAESP National Distinguished Principal
Central Elementary School
Cabot, AR

About the Authors

Barbara L. Brock is Associate Professor of Education at Creighton University in Omaha, Nebraska. She has held a variety of positions in education, including Education Department Chair, Director of School Administration, elementary principal, and K–12 teacher. She presents nationally and internationally on topics of beginning teacher induction, leadership succession, teacher and principal burnout, and educators with disabilities. She is coauthor with Marilyn Grady of five books, all published by Corwin Press: *Principals in Transition: Tips for Surviving Succession* (1995), *Rekindling the Flame: Principals Combating Teacher Burnout* (2000), *From First-Year to First-Rate: Principals Guiding New Teachers* (2nd ed., 2001), *Avoiding Burnout: A Principal's Guide to Keeping the Fire Alive* (2002), and *Launching Your First Principalship* (2004). She has also published articles in a number of journals, including *The Journal of the Mid-Western Research Association, Educational Considerations, Connections, Clearinghouse,* and *Catholic Education: A Journal of Inquiry and Practice.* She received her BA in art education from Briar Cliff University, an MS with a specialty in school administration from Creighton University, and an EdD in administration, curriculum, and instruction from the University of Nebraska-Lincoln.

Dr. Brock welcomes feedback and comments from readers. She can be reached by e-mail at bbrock@creighton.edu.

Marilyn L. Grady is Professor of Educational Administration at the University of Nebraska-Lincoln. She is the author or coauthor of 14 books. Her research areas include leadership, principalship, and superintendent-board relations. She has more than 150 articles to her credit.

She is the editor of the *Journal of Women in Educational Leadership* and has served on the editorial boards of *Educational Administration Quarterly, The Rural Educator, The Journal of At-Risk Issues, The Journal of School Leadership, Advancing Women in Leadership On-Line Journal,* and *The Journal for a Just and Caring Education.* She is the recipient of the Stanley Brzezinski Research Award and University of Nebraska-Lincoln's award for Outstanding Contributions to the Status of Women.

Dr. Grady coordinates an annual conference on women in educational leadership that attracts national attendance and is in its nineteenth year. She has served on the executive board of the National Council of Professors of Educational Administration, the Center for the Study of Small/Rural Schools, and Phi Delta Kappa Chapter 15. She is a member of the American Educational Research Association, the International Academy of Educational Leaders, the National Rural Education Association, the National Council of Professors of Educational Administration, the Association for Supervision and Curriculum Development, Phi Delta Kappa, and the Horace Mann League.

She has been an administrator in K–12 schools as well as at the college and university levels. She received her BA in history from Saint Mary's College, Notre Dame, Indiana, and her PhD in educational administration with a specialty in leadership from The Ohio State University.

Introduction

THE CHALLENGE

Never has the need to recruit and retain qualified new teachers been greater. Student populations are growing in number and diversity, and reform movements are demanding a higher quality of teaching. The growth of ethnic and minority student enrollment is creating a critical need for minority teachers. Rural and urban areas are experiencing steady growth in the number of English language learners, prompting a demand for teachers sensitive to the needs of non-native speakers (Lenhardt, 2000; NWREL, 1997).

Meanwhile, teacher attrition and retirements continue to increase and some areas of the nation are experiencing shortages of qualified teachers (RNT, 2000). A change in the way schools attract, develop, and retain new teachers is in order.

THE SOLUTION

An increasing number of school systems are recognizing the value of teacher induction programs in retaining and improving the performance of promising new teachers. Research has demonstrated that beginning teachers who receive support are more likely to remain in the teaching field. Equally important, new teachers who receive developmental assistance in their early years are more likely to develop effective teaching practices that endure throughout their careers (Brewster & Railsback, 2001; Moir, 2003).

Induction programs can assume many forms, ranging from short orientations to multiyear programs that provide developmental support as novice teachers progress. The induction program format suggested in this book is a multiyear developmental program that includes the components of orientation, mentoring, directed activities, seminars and workshops, and individualized, ongoing professional development. Individual schools' needs and contexts are viewed as central to selecting the format and content of the induction program.

The following factors, considered requisites for an effective induction program, are considered and explored throughout this book.

Effective teacher induction programs require

- Team effort
- Grounding in individual school needs and context
- A school environment conducive to student and teacher learning
- A comprehensive and developmental approach
- Adequate funding and resources
- An evaluation cycle

1

The Players

THE INDUCTION TEAM

The first step in creating a teacher induction program is assembling the team that is charged with designing the induction program. The team should include individuals who understand school and district needs as well as the needs of new teachers. Principals, teachers, union representatives, central office personnel, and university faculty can contribute to the teacher induction program.

The initiators of teacher induction programs may be staff development personnel or individual building principals. Subsequent ongoing management of an induction program might belong to a central office department, such as professional development or human resources, or an individual, such as an assistant superintendent, a consultant, a teacher on release time, or a building principal. The intended size and scope of the induction program often determines who initiates and ultimately who manages the program.

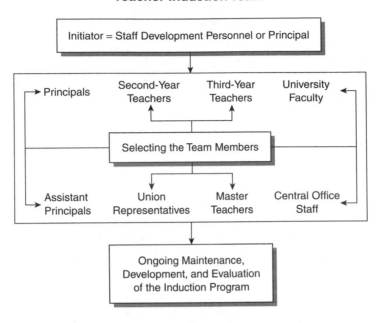

Teacher Induction Team

The Team's Role and Responsibilities

Regardless of who assumes responsibility for initiation, maintenance, development, and evaluation of an induction program, transforming a vision into an effective program requires committed leadership in each of the following areas:

1. Assessing school needs
2. Generating support from the school community
3. Designing the program
4. Monitoring progress
5. Evaluating the program

An important step is defining the extent of the induction team's responsibilities. Is the team responsible for program design only? If so, it must be decided who, when the program is ready for implementation, will be responsible for each of the following functions:

- Program implementation
- Program governance
- Budget
- Program maintenance
- Program development
- Program evaluation

THE PRINCIPAL

Building principals play a key role in the delivery, acceptance, and success of the induction program. Principals should be included in the program's design, know how to work with beginning teachers, and become key players in the delivery and evaluation of the induction program (Brock & Grady, 1998, 2001; Johnson, Freedman, Aschheim, & Krupp, 2003).

Principals need to understand the needs of new teachers and know how to assist them. New teachers report the importance of principals who provide encouragement, communicate clear expectations, observe classes, and offer feedback (Brock & Grady, 1998). Principals can remedy conditions that commonly contribute to new teacher failure (Ingersol & Smith, 2003): late appointments to teaching positions, improper teaching assignments, isolated classrooms, inadequate resources, failure to communicate expectations, and inadequate supervision (Brock & Grady 1998, 2001; Egan, 2002).

Critical responsibilities for principals in guiding entry-level teachers include

1. Making timely appointments to teaching positions that allow adequate preparation time

2. Making appropriate teaching assignments

3. Assigning a classroom near a mentor teacher

4. Providing adequate teaching resources

5. Communicating expectations for teaching and learning

6. Interacting with entry-level teachers individually and in small groups

7. Observing classroom teaching

8. Providing feedback and affirmation

THE SCHOOL COMMUNITY

Successful induction programs require the support and collaboration of the school community. Greater involvement leads to greater ownership of the program and its success. (Brock & Grady, 2001; Ganser, 2003). Invite the input, support, and cooperation of the members of the school community. Identify individuals who will be supportive as well as those who may be willing to provide assistance. Anticipate and curb potential sources of resistance.

Collaboration Resources

On the following form, name the individuals or groups who will be involved in developing the induction plan.

Collaboration Members	Names
Veteran Teachers	
Teacher Educators	
Principals	
Superintendents	
Central Office Supervisors	
School Board Members	
Local Education Association	
State Education Department	
State Education Association	
State Administrator Association	
Educational Service Unit	

Collaboration Involvements

Collegial support emerges when all participants perceive a need, agree on a purpose, and understand their roles and responsibilities (Sergiovanni, 2006). The leader should identify the participants and establish the framework for identifying the goals that will be achieved. The next step is to identify the roles and responsibilities of the group members. What will be the specific responsibilities of the following participants?

Collaboration Resources	Responsibilities
Veteran Teachers	
Teacher Educators	
Principals	
Superintendents	
Central Office Supervisors	
School Board Members	
Local Education Association	
State Education Department	
State Education Association	
State Administrator Association	
Educational Service Unit	

PROGRAM RECIPIENTS

School districts use many terms to describe the recipients of induction programs, such as *novice, entry level, beginning, new,* and *newly hired.* In this book, the term *new teacher* describes both inexperienced beginners and experienced, newly hired teachers. As you examine the following sections, identify the teachers who may benefit from the induction program, such as

Inexperienced, fully certified beginners

Inexperienced beginners in alternative certificate programs

Experienced teachers returning after an absence

Experienced teachers new to the district or school

Experienced teachers who request assistance

Experienced teachers who are on probation

Deterrents to Success

Research about new teachers identifies the problems that are common during the early years of teaching (Bolich, 2001; Brock & Grady, 1998, 2001). Although not all new teachers experience these problems, the frequency of their occurrence makes them worthy of consideration. Common sources of problems include inadequate preparation for teaching and workplace conditions, such as an inappropriate teaching assignment or a lack of support (Bolich, 2001; Brock & Grady, 2001). Workplace conditions are within the control of the principal, while other issues are candidates for inclusion in induction activities and new teacher assessment. Topics that should be addressed in the induction program include

- Subject knowledge
- Discipline
- Isolation
- Class size
- Teaching assignments
- Resources and/or equipment
- Extra duties
- Time management
- Language differences
- Diversity
- School culture
- School morale
- Working conditions
- Special needs students

New teachers agree that their problems are avoidable if these needs are met:

- An appropriate teaching assignment
- Adequate resources
- A mentor
- Observations and feedback from the principal
- A climate of support among the faculty
- Assistance related to their needs

Unique Needs

New teachers have varied backgrounds, educational experiences, skills, and learning styles; consequently, their rate of development and needs are different (Brock & Grady, 2001; Ganser, 2003). These differences must be acknowledged throughout the teacher induction program. The content and delivery of the teacher induction program must be tailored to meet these unique needs. Consider how the needs of the following individuals may vary:

A traditional graduate of a teacher education program

A nontraditional graduate of a teacher education program

An individual entering the teaching field after leaving a different career

An experienced teacher returning to teaching

An individual who completed an alternative certification program

An experienced teacher moving to a new school

An experienced teacher changing grade levels or subject areas

There will be needs shared by all of these individuals. There also will be unique individual needs that must be identified. The induction program must address and meet all of these needs.

To keep the induction program content current and relevant, it is important to conduct periodic assessments to identify the needs of the teachers and potential problem areas. Assessments should be completed before school begins and at least once each quarter throughout the year. Although new teachers should be the primary source of data, additional sources might include mentors, veteran teachers, and the principal. Needs shift as new teachers progress from the "survival" stage to more advanced levels of instructional concern. It is important to anticipate and provide advance assistance for situations that routinely arise throughout the school year.

KEY IDEAS

A first step is to identify the members of the induction team. Once these players are identified, determine individual roles and responsibilities. Enlist the support and collaboration of the school community so that there is greater ownership of the program. Identify the specific individuals who will be program beneficiaries. Tailor the program to the specific and unique needs of these teachers.

2

Current Problems:
Past Practices

CURRENT PROBLEMS

Teacher induction programs often emerge to solve problems with new teacher retention or teacher performance. An essential first step in designing a new teacher induction program is assessing past practices. Although teacher turnover or teaching problems may be apparent, the source of these problems may not be clear. An assessment of current problems and past practices provides a more complete understanding and subsequently a more accurate solution to existing challenges.

Dissatisfaction with current practices of teacher induction may tempt one to "throw out" everything that has been attempted in the past and to start over again. It may seem as though nothing was effective. However, a more prudent strategy is to assess past strategies and retain those that were successful.

What are the current induction problems? For each problem, diagnose the underlying causes and examine past induction practices. Sources of assessment data may include

- Statistics on teacher attrition
- New teacher performance evaluations
- Feedback from new teachers
- Feedback from mentors
- Principal observations
- Student evaluations
- Teacher exit interviews

For best results, obtain assessment feedback from as many sources as possible.

Attrition

Teacher attrition is costly in terms of student learning and finances. High teacher turnover disrupts student learning, destroys continuity (Ingersol & Smith, 2003), weakens tradition, and diminishes the school's reputation. Continual recruiting, interviewing, hiring, and induction contribute to the school's financial burdens and require a significant investment of time (Moir, 2003).

Induction programs can improve the teacher retention rate when the causes of attrition are understood and strategies are implemented to alleviate contributing problems. Identifying the rate and causes of attrition are the first steps in identifying solutions (Bolich, 2001; Ingersol & Smith, 2003). The following exercises will assist you with this task.

New Teacher Attrition: Beginning Teachers

1. During the last three years, how many beginning teachers (with less than three years of experience) left the school?

2. Name the beginning teachers who left.

3. Of these teachers, how many left the teaching profession?

4. Of these teachers, how many transferred to another school?

5. Of these teachers, how many left based on your recommendation?

6. Of the departures that were due to your recommendation, what were the teachers' difficulties?

7. Of the teachers who left because of your recommendation, how many did you hire?

8. What strategies did you use to improve the teachers' performance?

9. Of the total number of teachers who left, how many departures were the choice of the teachers?

10. Of the total number of teachers who left, how many did you hire?

11. Describe the characteristics of the teachers who left during their first three years.

12. What were the most common difficulties that the "leavers" displayed?

New Teacher Attrition: Experienced Teachers, New to School

1. During the last three years, how many beginning teachers (with less than three years of experience) left the school?

2. Name the beginning teachers who left.

3. Of these teachers, how many left the teaching profession?

4. Of these teachers, how many transferred to another school?

5. Of these teachers, how many left based on your recommendation?

6. Of the departures that were due to your recommendation, what were the teachers' difficulties?

7. Of the teachers who left because of your recommendation, how many did you hire?

8. What strategies did you use to improve the teachers' performance?

9. Of the total number of teachers who left, how many departures were the choice of the teachers?

10. Of the total number of teachers who left, how many did you hire?

11. Describe the characteristics of the teachers who left during their first three years.

12. What were the most common difficulties that the "leavers" displayed?

PAST PRACTICE

Retention Efforts

Before discarding past retention efforts, consider them based on the information about attrition and determine their degree of success. Some past efforts may be worth retaining or revising.

Retaining Quality Teachers

Consider the following questions:

- What have been your successes in retaining quality teachers?

- What actions did you take to retain quality teachers?

- What challenges have you experienced in attempting to retain quality teachers?

- Whose assistance do you need in retaining quality teachers?

- What resources do you need to retain quality teachers?

Enhancing the Professional Competence and Instructional Ability of Teachers

Consider the following questions:

- What actions have you taken to improve the *competence* of first-year teachers?

- What challenges have you experienced related to the *competence* of first-year teachers?

- What assistance do you need in improving teacher *competence?*

- What actions have you taken to improve the *instructional ability* of first-year teachers?

- What challenges have you experienced related to the *instructional ability* of first-year teachers?

- What assistance do you need in improving teachers' *instructional ability?*

Improving the School Climate by Stimulating the Professional Growth of the Faculty

Consider the following questions:

- What actions have you taken to create a positive school climate?

- How do you encourage the professional growth of teachers?

New Teacher Performance

All new teachers want to succeed. They begin their careers with enthusiasm and expectations for success. However, preservice education does not prepare new teachers to assume the same responsibilities as veteran teachers. New teachers, like newcomers in any profession, require assistance and support throughout their initial years (Brock & Grady, 2001).

During the early months of teaching, new teachers typically focus on daily survival. Their goal is preparing lessons for the day and maintaining order in their classrooms. The effectiveness of their teaching strategies on student performance is not yet the main consideration (Glickman, Gordon, & Ross-Gordon, 2004). Without the infusion of new ideas and strategies during the formative years, initial "survival strategies" become entrenched, often adopted for a lifetime.

Although all new teachers want to perform well, many are plagued with performance problems. The source of their difficulties may stem from a variety of issues, such as immaturity, lack of teaching experience, inadequate educational preparation, workplace conditions, and/or newness of the school culture.

The first step in a solution is an accurate identification of the problem's source. When symptoms of a behavior are addressed but the possible underlying causes are not, the problem continues to grow and fester. For instance, consider the multiple causes of classroom discipline problems. Problems may stem from poorly designed lessons, lack of knowledge of classroom management, or inconsistent practices (Larrivee, 2005).

The following exercises focus on new teacher performance and past efforts to improve performance.

New Teacher Performance: Diagnosing Performance Problems

Consider the problems of newly hired teachers and match them with an underlying source. Note how you have responded to these problems and the results of your actions.

Possible Sources	Manifestations of Problems	Your Response to the Problem	Results
Immaturity			
Lack of teaching experience			
Inadequate educational preparation			
New school culture			
Other sources (specify)			

Performance and New Teachers

In which of the following areas do new teachers in your building need assistance? (Check all that apply.)

Performance Areas	✓	Describe the Needs
Classroom management		
Working with students		
Working with parents		
Working with peers		
Lesson planning		
Instructional strategies		
Curriculum development		
Professionalism		
Communicating		
Organizational skills		

Performance Areas	✓	Describe the Needs
Adjusting to the role of teacher		
Adjusting to the school		
Meeting team expectations		
Adhering to school policies		
Managing time		
Grading student work		
Meeting educational standards		
Balancing professional and personal roles		
Meeting student needs		
Working with diverse student needs		

Improving Performance

Consider the actions you have taken to improve the performance of entry-level teachers.

Enhancing Performance and Instructional Ability

- What actions have you taken to improve the *performance* of first-year teachers?

- What challenges have you experienced in attempting to improve teacher *performance?*

- What assistance do you need to improve teacher *performance?*

- What specific expertise should you enlist to enhance teacher *performance?*

Past Induction Efforts

Consider the beginning teacher induction or assistance you have offered in the past. Instead of discarding previous efforts, determine which ones were effective and worth maintaining, which ones need modification, and which ones need elimination. Identify new strategies that may be successful.

Past Induction Efforts

On the following form, place a check mark (✔) next to the strategies used and briefly describe each. Indicate your satisfaction with each strategy in the column on the right by marking it satisfactory (S) or unsatisfactory (U). Use this assessment to identify the strategies that should be retained in your beginning teacher induction program.

Strategies Used	✓	Descriptions	Satisfactory (S)	Unsatisfactory (U)
Orientation				
Mentor program				
Seminars				
Orientation				
Mentor program				
Seminars				
Workshops				
Modeling by mentors				

(Continued)

Strategies Used	✓	Descriptions	Satisfactory (S)	Unsatisfactory (U)
Meetings with principal				
Required shadowing				
Classroom visits at other schools				
Observations and/or feedback				
Other strategies (specify)				

KEY IDEAS

An assessment of current problems and past practices provides a database for the development of an induction program. The ideal is to retain successful practices and address problem areas. Among the considerations are attrition and retention, competence, instructional skill, school climate, performance issues, and past induction strategies.

3

Program Evaluation

An evaluation plan should be developed in conjunction with the needs assessment to guide all induction activities. Evaluating the induction program is vital to its effectiveness and success. The evaluation should involve all constituents and include both formative and summative dimensions. Formative evaluation is an ongoing process that occurs throughout the program and encourages constant adjustments to align the program with its intended outcomes. Summative evaluation occurs at the end of a program cycle to determine the value of the program, to identify needed changes, to provide information for stakeholders, and in some states, to satisfy mandates for beginning teacher assistance programs. The steps in the evaluation cycle include

- Initial assessment
- Goal identification
- Planned activities
- Activity assessment
- Semester and yearly evaluation

INITIAL ASSESSMENT

The needs assessment provides the baseline for initial planning of the induction program. Initial assessment involves gathering data from multiple sources prior to goal identification. The following exercises may be helpful in assessing the school culture, work environment, and new teacher needs.

Culture

Describe the cultural uniqueness of your school, community, and people.

1. What are the *cultural characteristics of the school*?

2. What are the *cultural characteristics of the community*?

3. What are the *unique characteristics* of the people in the community?

The Work Environment

Which of these conditions are present in the school? (Check all that apply.)

Conditions	✓
Mutual respect of novice and instructor	
Collaboration among peers	
Mutual trust within the staff	
Supportiveness of peers and administrators	
Openness and authenticity of expression	
Pleasurable learning experiences	
A comfortable and accepting atmosphere	

Areas of Need

Which of the following needs do new teachers demonstrate? (Check all that apply.)

Areas of Need	✓
Discipline and classroom management	
Emotional support	
Responding to varying levels of student abilities	
Planning, organization, and time management	
Communicating with students, parents, faculty, and administration	
Assessing students' work	
Understanding the procedures and policies of the school	
Adjusting to the teaching profession	
Obtaining resources	
Using effective teaching strategies	

Identifying Needs

How does each of the following contribute to your understanding of the needs of first-year teachers in the school?

Research:

Preparation programs:

The profession:

(Continued)

Second-year teachers:

Mentors:

Principals:

Experienced teachers:

First-year teachers:

GOALS AND ACTIVITIES

Program goals derive from the results of the needs assessment and provide the basis for program development and evaluation. Once goals are determined, the next step is to identify specific activities to achieve the goals and individuals who will be responsible for the activities.

ACTIVITY ASSESSMENT

Each activity should include an evaluation component that will guide future planning. Data are gathered at regular intervals to reveal the changing needs of new teachers and determine the effectiveness of program activities.

Assessment

Indicate how each of the following items will be assessed.

Program design:

Program leadership:

Mentor selection:

Mentor assignment:

Mentor training:

Mentor performance:

Orientation:

Seminars:

Classroom observations:

Direct assistance:

PROGRAM EVALUATION

A summative program evaluation should be conducted annually to determine the future direction of the program. The following questions, based on Glickman and colleagues' (2004) components of program evaluation, are useful in evaluating an induction program.

Evaluation

1. Was there a need for an induction program?

2. Were the program goals and activities consistent with the needs? If not, what changes are required?

3. Were adequate human and material resources dedicated to the program? If not, what additional resources are needed?

4. Were stakeholders ready to support implementation of the program? If not, how can the situation be remedied?

5. Was the program implemented as planned? If not, why not?

6. Did the program meet its intended outcomes? If not, what outcomes remain unmet?

7. What were the unintended outcomes of the program?

8. Were program benefits commensurate with human and material expenditures? If not, what caused a disparity in the ratio?

GATHERING DATA

New teachers, their mentors, other faculty members, students, parents, principals, and classroom products are potential sources of data for both formative and summative evaluation. Methods of gathering evaluation data include surveys, interviews, observations, systematic review of classroom products, and longitudinal studies of new teachers' progress. Determine in advance the kinds of data to gather and the mechanisms that will be used to evaluate the data.

Evaluation Data

The sources of data, the types of data, and how the data will be collected should be planned before the program begins. Using the following list as a guide, consider what data will be collected and how they will be collected.

Indicators of student learning

What:

How:

First-year teacher feedback

What:

How:

Observation data

What:

How:

(Continued)

Postactivity feedback

What:

How:

Survey data

What:

How:

Mentor feedback

What:

How:

Student feedback

What:

How:

Parent feedback

What:

How:

Principal feedback

What:

How:

THE EVALUATORS

Decide who will conduct the formative and summative assessments. The evaluators may include members of the central office staff, the principal, the team that designed the program, and/or an outside consultant. Everyone who has a stake in the program should be included in the process and informed of the outcomes.

THE EVALUATION CYCLE

The evaluation cycle is depicted below and followed by questions to help you prepare for it.

The Evaluation Cycle

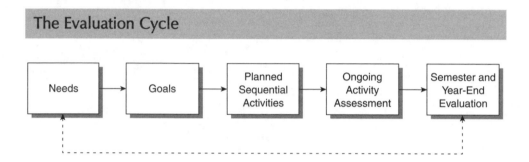

1. What are the induction needs of first-year teachers?

2. What are the goals for the induction program?

3. What are the planned sequential activities that will occur during the year?

4. How will each of the activities be assessed?

5. What semester and year-end evaluations will be conducted? (Brock & Grady, 2001)

SHARING RESULTS

Individuals responsible for making program decisions need a detailed report of all aspects of the evaluation. Stakeholders should receive a summary of findings, conclusions, and decisions that will affect them. The report, in its entirety, should be available to all stakeholders who want to review it. The evaluation report should include the following components:

- The purpose of the evaluation (initial assessment, activity assessment, summative evaluation)
- A description of the induction program (within the context of the school)
- Evaluation questions
- The methodology (data-gathering processes, subjects, analysis, time frame)
- Results and conclusions
- Recommendations for the future (Glickman et al., 2004)

EVALUATION OF NEW TEACHERS

If a goal of the induction program is to improve new teacher performance, then assessment of teacher growth should be an integral part of the evaluation. Assessment of the performance of individual teachers should include both formative assessment, for purposes of their growth, and summative evaluation, for determining whether or not to continue their employment.

Some school districts are linking induction programs with the evaluation of new teachers. For those interested in finding out more about the topic, the following state induction programs provide contrasting models of assistance: California's Beginning Teacher Support and Assessment Program, Connecticut's Beginning Educator Support and Training Program, and Ohio's programs in Toledo, Cincinnati, and Columbus (Feiman-Nemser, Carver, Schwille, & Yusko, 1999).

Other school districts choose to view induction and appraisal as related, yet independent, functions. Formative assessments, accompanied by constructive feedback, are viewed as vital to new teacher learning and development. Mentors and administrators are encouraged to conduct informal, formative assessments as part of the learning process. However, formal appraisals, to determine ongoing employment, remain in the province of the school's administrator.

Regardless of the form of assessment, the process and respective roles of participants should be clearly defined. Teacher performance standards should be linked with district and state standards (Fideler & Haselkorn, 1999) and grounded in a vision of what constitutes good teaching. Professional teaching standards, such as those developed by the Interstate New Teacher Assessment and Support Consortium (1996), may be useful in developing that vision.

KEY IDEAS

A program evaluation plan should be developed in conjunction with the initial needs assessment. Evaluation should be both formative and summative. The steps in the evaluation cycle include initial assessment, goal identification, planned activities, activity assessment, and semester and yearly evaluation. A timeline for evaluation activities should be established. Individual responsibilities for evaluation tasks should be specified.

4

School Culture

A developmental induction program is defined, in part, by the contextual demands and constraints of the school culture. A positive and productive school culture is essential to an effective induction program. Even the best induction program will languish in a troubled school culture (Brock & Grady, 2001; Ganser, 2003).

CHARACTERISTICS OF SCHOOL CULTURE

Planning an induction program presents an excellent opportunity to examine the nuances of school culture. One way to ensure that the culture remains positive and productive is through a periodic examination of the attitudes, traditions, and routines that have shaped it. Each school and school district is a unique entity imbued with a culture that emerged through years of members' interactions with each other and the school community. Cultures form when behaviors and practices, adopted to meet specific needs, perpetuate (Cole, 1991; Deal & Peterson, 1990; Sergiovanni, 2006). Sometimes behaviors and practices that once served a purpose continue even though the need no longer exists (Owens, 1995). Although some traditions, attitudes, and routine behaviors continue to be useful, others may become undesirable, even harmful to the school's performance.

A second reason to examine school culture is to assist new teachers in understanding it. The nuances of a school's culture often pose problems for new teachers. These reasons account for their struggles:

- School culture is unwritten, making it difficult for newcomers to learn.
- Some school cultures do not welcome newcomers.
- The school culture and the teacher may not be a good match (Brock & Grady, 2001).

IMPACT OF SCHOOL CULTURE

Given the impact of a school's culture on new teacher success, an assessment of the prevailing culture is critical. Four levels of culture exist in most schools (Hart & Bredeson, 1996):

1. Cultural elements common to schools in general

2. Cultural elements characteristic of a particular school or community, such as demographic issues
   - How does the rural, suburban, or urban setting of the school affect its culture?
   - Does the district employ adequate numbers of teachers?
   - Are the building, grounds, and resources adequate?
   - Does the school hire teachers who are fully qualified or teachers who are learning to teach "on the job"?
   - What is the turnover rate and what is the ratio of experienced to inexperienced teachers?
   - Is the community supportive of the school?

3. Cultural elements unique to the people who compose the school community
   - What part do socioeconomic, linguistic, and cultural factors play in the school?
   - Do the teachers and students share a common socioeconomic and cultural background?
   - How many of the students are English Language Learners?
   - What languages do students speak at home?
   - What is the attitude of the teachers to the students and their parents?

- What is the attitude of students and parents to teachers and education?
- What expectations do parents have for the teachers and school?

4. Cultural elements common to a specific kind of school
   - What makes the school unique?
   - Is it a magnet school?
   - Does it have a religious affiliation?

Demographic features of a school and community deserve increased attention by school professionals. Societal changes may be seemingly "invisible" unless attention is given to current census data (Grady, in press).

Schools with a religious affiliation have a culture governed, largely, by values espoused by that religion. The school's mission, goals, methods, and curriculum reflect the religious nature of the school. Requirements for teachers in nonpublic schools are often different than for teachers in public schools. Expectations for teaching religion, infusing religious values into curriculum, and participating in religious functions are not addressed in secular teacher preparation programs. Thus, principals should not assume the preparedness of new teachers for the religious culture of the school (Brock, 1988; Brock & Grady, 2000; Chatlain, 2002).

The exercise that follows provides a guide for principals and teachers to use in examining the relationship among the school's culture, the existing workplace environment, and the socialization of newly hired teachers. Look at the school as an outsider might see it. The exercise will yield information that can be used to help new teachers learn more about the school's culture and the students' unique learning needs.

School Culture

Respond to each of these questions:

1. What are the *characteristics of the school culture?*

2. What are the *cultural characteristics of the school community?*

3. What are the *unique characteristics* of the people in the community?

A CULTURE OF PROFESSIONAL GROWTH

Learning to teach is a lifelong process, one that begins at the preservice level and continues throughout a teaching career. The time spent in preservice studies is extremely short compared to the length of a teaching career. Consequently, the learning that occurs "on the job" plays a critical role in determining the quality of a teacher's performance.

Although teachers have individual responsibility for pursuing professional growth, how actively they do so is influenced by the school culture in which they work (Sergiovanni & Starratt, 2002). New teachers follow the expectations of the culture to which they are exposed. Those who begin their careers in a culture that supports and encourages professional growth will likely adopt high standards for continuous learning.

School culture manifests itself in the work environment of teachers (Brock & Grady, 2001; Peterson, 1999). Unspoken norms, so much a part of the culture that members are unconscious of their existence, drive teacher behaviors. For instance, some school cultures promote a workaholic atmosphere in which teachers feel compelled to work excessive hours to the detriment of their personal lives. At the opposite extreme is the lackadaisical culture in which teachers barely meet contractual obligations, much less pursue professional growth. Ideally, principals strive for a work culture that encourages teachers to establish a balance between professional and personal lives.

Cultural norms also drive the degree of collegiality and professional growth that occurs in a school (Peterson, 1999; Sergiovanni & Starratt, 2002). Knowing that new teachers are more likely to thrive when welcomed into a supportive environment, principals must foster a supportive environment in which a culture of collegiality and continuous development flourishes. Characteristics of supportive school cultures include open communication, trust, and mutual respect.

A Supportive Work Environment

How are each of the following nurtured in the school?

Mutual respect of first-year teacher and mentor:

Collaboration among peers:

Trust within the staff:

Supportive peers and administrators:

Openness and authenticity of expression:

Pleasurable learning experiences:

A CULTURE OF COLLEGIALITY

Although a collaborative teaching environment is highly desirable, it seldom develops by accident. A culture of collegiality must be advocated and supported by the principal (Glickman, Gordon, & Ross-Gordon, 2005; Peterson, 1999; Sergiovanni & Starratt, 2002). Deterrents to collegiality include the isolated nature of teaching that encourages teachers to develop private and idiosyncratic approaches to teaching. In addition, an atmosphere of distrust among teachers and administration encourages competition rather than collaboration.

Principals can promote collegiality through the following practices:

- Stating expectations for collegiality
- Collaborating with faculty in making school improvements
- Providing recognition, funding, materials, or space to teachers who collaborate
- Supporting teachers as they engage in collegial behaviors (Barth, 1990; Cole, 1993).

Collegiality

How do your actions support collegiality? Describe your current practices.

- How often do you state expectations for collegiality?

- How do you emphasize the importance of collegiality in the school?

- How do you encourage collaboration in making school improvements?

- What recognition, funding, materials, or space have you provided for teachers who collaborate?

- How do you support teachers who demonstrate collegial behaviors?

Continuous professional development is most likely to occur when the following conditions are present:

- Teachers are reflective and engaged in frequent, continuous talk about teaching practice.
- Teachers try out new techniques in the classroom (Leithwood, 1990).
- Teachers are frequently observed and provided with useful feedback about their teaching.
- Teachers communicate regularly and openly with the principal.
- Teachers collaborate with other teachers in school improvement activities (Raywid, 1993).
- Teachers design, prepare, and evaluate teaching materials together.
- Teachers teach each other the art of teaching (Little, 1982).

Assessing the Culture for Professional Growth Practices

How does the culture of the school support continuous professional development? Does a culture of collegiality exist? Which of these conditions are present? (Check all that apply.)

Conditions	✓
Teachers reflecting on their practice	
Teachers engaged in frequent, continuous talk about teaching practices	
Teachers trying out new techniques and practices	
Teachers observed and provided with feedback about their teaching on a regular basis	
Teachers visiting with the principal to discuss new ideas or teaching concerns	
Teachers designing, preparing, and evaluating teaching materials together	
Teachers collaborating for school improvement	
Teachers teaching each other the art of teaching	

Creating Conditions for Professional Growth

What steps will you take to create the following conditions for professional growth in the school?

Teachers reflecting on their practice:

Teachers engaged in frequent, continuous talk about teaching practices:

Teachers trying out new techniques and practices:

Teachers observed and provided with feedback about their teaching on a regular basis:

Teachers visiting with the principal to discuss new ideas or teaching concerns:

Teachers designing, preparing, and evaluating teaching materials together:

Teachers collaborating for school improvement:

Teachers teaching each other the art of teaching:

KEY IDEAS

A positive and productive school culture is essential to an effective induction program. A periodic examination of the attitudes, traditions, and routines in the school is a means of maintaining a positive culture. School and community demographics are important contributors to school culture. A positive culture of professional growth and collegiality supports the work of teachers.

5

Program Foundation

Once you have assessed current induction problems, past induction practices, and school culture, you should understand what the induction program needs to accomplish and how to structure the program. This chapter is a guide to developing the foundation for an induction program.

DEVELOPMENTAL TEACHER INDUCTION

A developmental teacher induction program is based on a sequenced set of professional growth activities that provide support and assistance to new teachers throughout their induction years. Developmental induction programs are based on adult learning theory that suggests change occurs when individuals perceive a need for improvement and choose to pursue actions that lead to improvement (Knowles, 1980). In such programs, assistance is individually prescribed according to each teacher's perception of need rather than by a predetermined notion of what new teachers need to know. Teachers are encouraged to attempt innovative teaching and develop a personalized style of teaching rather than a prescribed style (Brock & Grady, 2001).

Induction programs that are developmental have as their basis a shared philosophy and well-defined goals that are oriented to meet the situational needs of beginning teachers within the contextual demands and constraints of individual schools (Brock & Grady, 2001; Runyan, 1991). The programs provide continuous support in a collegial, supportive environment. A prerequisite to their success is a healthy school culture (Brock & Grady, 2001; Dilworth & Imig, 1995).

PHILOSOPHY

The philosophy of the individuals who design the teacher induction program is a determining factor in how the program will be perceived, structured, and developed. People act on what they believe. Members of the design team need to examine their individual beliefs, determine core values, and agree on a shared vision early in the design phase.

Assumptions to consider include the following philosophical orientations:

- New teachers possess basic skills and strive to become good teachers.
- New teachers seek opportunities to learn when they perceive a need and have a desire to change.
- Induction is a multiyear developmental process that bridges preservice training through career-long development.

Philosophical Foundations

Using the following guidelines, describe the philosophy, goals, and structure of your induction program.

- A developmental philosophy for new teachers

- Goals for first-year teachers tailored to the school

- The structure that provides year-round support for new teachers, beginning with an orientation before school begins and continuing throughout the induction period

RATIONALE

A number of concerns, such as the following, may have prompted the creation of the induction program.

- Retaining quality teachers
- Enhancing instructional performance
- Stimulating professional growth for the faculty

The rationale for the induction program may be the resolution of one concern or a combination of these concerns. The answers to the following questions provide the rationale and goals for the teacher induction program.

1. Why does the school or district need a teacher induction program?

2. What problems will be resolved by the teacher induction program?

The Rationale for the Teacher Induction Program

Based on the information you have about the teachers and the school, state the rationale for your teacher induction program in the space provided.

GOALS

Goals derive from the philosophical basis and rationale of the program. Factors influencing the goals and the size and scope of the program include the school's size, structure, and availability of financial resources. Possible program goals may include the following:

- Retaining quality teachers
- Providing emotional support to new teachers
- Supplementing teachers' knowledge and instructional skills
- Encouraging professional attitudes
- Encouraging concern for students
- Encouraging creative and innovative teaching
- Promoting development of individualized teaching styles
- Improving teaching performance
- Initiating teachers' continuous professional growth
- Promoting the professional growth of the entire faculty

Induction programs should not be considered the panacea for retaining and developing quality teachers. Some problems experienced by new teachers cannot be solved solely by an induction program (Ganser, 2003). Induction programs cannot

- Eliminate problems inherent in transitioning to a new profession
- Improve teacher retention or performance in troubled school environments
- Improve the functioning of a teacher who lacks the ability to be a teacher

State the goals for your induction program in the following exercise.

Program Goals

Which of the following are goals for your induction program? (Check all that apply.)

Goal	✓
Providing a transition from preservice preparation through the first year of teaching	
Promoting the personal and professional well-being of beginning teachers	
Retaining competent teachers	
Providing additional knowledge and skills	
Encouraging professional attitudes	
Assisting beginning teachers with their needs and concerns	
Building a foundation for teachers' continued professional growth through structured contact with mentors, administrators, and veteran teachers	
Helping beginning teachers develop their own self-image, positive attitude, and concern for students	
Encouraging creative and innovative teaching	
Improving teaching performance	

STRATEGIES

Developmental induction programs provide ongoing support throughout the induction period. Program strategies vary according to program goals, resources and expertise, and new teachers' needs. The following strategies are commonly used.

- *Orientation* to welcome and explain information about the school and district policies and procedures
- *School and district information kits* to provide written information about the school and school district
- *Mentor programs* to have trained mentors assist novices throughout the induction period
- *Socialization opportunities* to welcome and acquaint the newcomer with school personnel
- *Observations and feedback from principal* to assist the newcomer in meeting performance expectations and in establishing continuous dialogue with the principal
- *Ongoing assistance* to provide ongoing opportunities that vary according to new teachers' needs, including
  - Observation of peer teaching
  - Informal interactions with principal or supervisor
  - Direct assistance with problems
  - New teacher meetings and seminars
  - Newsletters and books for new teachers
  - Systematic plans for individual professional development
  - Portfolio development

Induction Program Activities

In the following exercise, identify the induction activities that exist in your school and indicate how the success of each activity will be evaluated. (Check all that apply.)

Activity	✓	Method of Evaluation
Mentor selection		
Mentor assignment		
Meetings with mentors		
Orientation sessions		
Observations of peer teaching		
Formal meetings with teachers		
Informal meetings with teachers		
Interviews with first-year teachers		
Seminars		
Information kits		
Informal socialization opportunities		
Formal socialization opportunities		
Principal and/or supervisor observations and feedback		
Individual professional development plan meetings		
Portfolio development sessions		

FINANCIAL SUPPORT

Providing a financial base for the induction program is critical to the program's longevity. An induction program is more likely to become a permanent program if it is funded through a school or school district's annual budget.

Most schools or school districts finance induction programs at the local level through annual operating budgets. Some states mandate induction programs and provide matching funds or start-up funds. Grants may be available to fund the programs. As funding opportunities vary, investigating information on availability of state funds and grants is advisable.

The next two exercises concern calculating operating costs and identifying funding sources.

Calculating Costs

Consider the number and scope of the program components you plan to incorporate and estimate the cost of each.

Component	Estimated Cost
Induction program coordinator	
• Salary or stipend	
• Release time	
• Training	
• Resources	
• Technology	
Orientation	
• Refreshments	
• Materials	
• Speakers	
• Teacher stipends for extra hours or days	

(Continued)

Component	Estimated Cost
Mentor program	
• Salaries or stipends	
• Release time	
• Training	
• Substitute teachers	
Peer observation	
• Substitute teachers	
Seminars or workshops	
• Room rental	
• Materials	
• Technology	
• Refreshments	
• Speaker stipends or travel expenses	
• Substitute teachers	
Classes, training, conferences	
• Registration	
• Travel expenses	
• Substitute teachers	
• Course materials	
Additional components	
•	
•	
•	

Funding the Induction Program

What are the potential funding sources for your school's induction program? Identify the sources in the spaces provided.

Funding Sources

School budget:

State assistance:

Grants:

Foundations:

Innovation—incentive funds:

Other:

KEY IDEAS

A developmental teacher induction program is based on a sequenced set of professional growth activities. A shared philosophy, well-defined goals, and adult learning theory are essential elements of the program. A variety of strategies and activities are available to program developers, including orientations, information kits, mentors, socialization opportunities, observation and feedback, as well as needs-based activities. Determining essential resources for development activities is a critical consideration.

6

The Orientation Component

The orientation component addresses issues critical to new teachers during the first part of the school year and should be considered the first phase of an induction program. New teacher assistance needs are divided into issues that are critical early in the year and those that surface once the school year is under way.

Since teachers arc eager to learn about their new responsibilities, orientation should begin after contract signing and continue throughout the early weeks of the school year. The orientation process involves both individual and group meetings, with the number of scheduled meeting days varying from as few as one day to five or more days. Providing several brief orientation sessions before school begins and follow-up meetings throughout the year may offer the best opportunity to avoid giving teachers information overload. Information disseminated during brief periods interspersed with time for questions and reflection is more likely to be understood and remembered.

The following components should be included in the orientation:

- Assignment of a contact person or assistance team
- School and district information kits
- Assignment of mentors
- Socialization opportunities
- Informal interactions between teachers and the principal or supervisor
- New teacher meetings and seminars
- Newsletters and books written specifically for new teachers

THE CONTACT PERSON

The signing of the contract is the beginning of the orientation period. After contract signing, teachers need a knowledgeable contact person who can answer questions and assist with personal concerns. The type and amount of support needed depend on the teacher's age, experience, and familiarity with the area. Teachers who are relocating may need assistance with the practical concerns of a move to an unfamiliar city, such as locating residences, banks, physicians, dentists, and day cares, and obtaining drivers' licenses. If the school district does not assign a liaison to assist newcomers with personal concerns, the duty to appoint one rests with the principal.

The Contact Person

The following exercise focuses on the selection of the contact person and expectations of that person. Consider the following questions.

- How will contact persons be assigned?

- What will the contact person's responsibilities include?

- Which of the following tasks will the contact person be responsible for? (Check all that apply.)

Tasks	✓
A welcoming phone call	
A personal meeting	
One or more question and answer sessions	
A tour of the neighborhood, city	
Relocation assistance	
Introductions to colleagues	

ORIENTATION MEETINGS

The purpose of orientation is to provide new teachers with enough information to ensure their success. The more time that is devoted to orientation activities and the more welcome teachers feel, the more likely it is that teachers will have a successful first year.

Schools typically spend from one to five days providing initial orientation, socialization opportunities, and time for new teachers to work in the classrooms. Throughout the year, additional meetings and seminars are scheduled to follow up on information and address emerging developmental needs of the new teachers. Socialization opportunities are an important component of meetings, as they encourage new friendships and ease the newcomer's transition. In addition, some school districts provide each inexperienced teacher with a book on beginning a teaching career. Schools also provide monthly beginning teacher newsletters.

THE OPENING MEETING

The following topics should be included in the opening orientation meeting:

- Welcome the new teachers.
- Introduce all individuals who are present.
- Distribute a directory of school employees that includes photos of the employees.
- Provide written information about the school and school district.
- Distribute photo ID cards to the teachers.
- Based on the size of the group, facilitate an "icebreaker" or "get acquainted" activity.
- Introduce teachers to their mentors.
- Describe a schedule for orientation activities.
- Describe the assistance available to teachers in the school.
- Provide class lists.
- Highlight the mission of the school, the goals for the year, and the expectations for student learning and teacher performance.
- Explain how and where to obtain teaching resources.
- Describe procedures for obtaining services.
- Provide time for socialization and refreshments.
- Provide a tour of the school.
- Show teachers their classrooms.
- Allow time during each orientation day for teachers to work in their classrooms.

Preparation for the Opening Meeting

Consider how you will conduct the opening meeting as you respond to each of these questions.

Introductions of the Faculty and Staff

- How will introductions be made?

- How will introductions at the opening orientation meeting be made memorable for those in attendance?

- How will technology be incorporated into the introductions?

- Does a school directory with photos exist? If not, who will assemble this information?

Icebreaker

- Which icebreaker activity would be best suited for the opening meeting?

- How many individuals will be involved in the activity?

- What room setup arrangements will facilitate the icebreaker and the opening meeting?

(Continued)

Mentor-New Teacher Matches

- How will the mentor-new teacher matches be made?

- What preparation will the mentors receive prior to the opening meeting?

- What will be the mentors' responsibilities during orientation?

Location of Resources

- What materials and resources will first-year teachers need?

- How do teachers access these materials and resources?

- What guide will be provided so that teachers will be able to locate resources throughout the year?

- Who will develop the guide and what should be included in it?

Procedures for Obtaining Clerical, Custodial, and Maintenance Services

- Who are the key persons in each of these areas?

- Where are they located?

- What specific services will each of these persons provide to first-year teachers?

- What forms must be completed to request services?

- Where are these forms located?

Socialization Time

- Who will be present?

- How will interaction be encouraged?

- What refreshments will be provided?

A Tour of the School

- Who will conduct the tour?

- What should be included in the tour?

TOPICS FOR ORIENTATION

Schools generally schedule from one to five orientation meetings for new teachers. Topics for the meetings should be prioritized according to the number of days available and divided into small meaningful increments. Providing information incrementally increases the probability of teachers' understanding and retaining it. Providing too much information at one time may be overwhelming and the information may be forgotten.

At the end of each meeting, distribute an information packet concerning the topics discussed and introduce the topics that will be presented at the next meeting. This will provide teachers with the time to reflect on what they have learned and may suggest questions to be raised at the next meeting.

In addition to the topics identified in the following exercises, some schools schedule a series of workshops held during the first three years that reinforce orientation topics (Sargent, 2003), such as discipline, diversity, and special education. The next three exercises address considerations for the initial orientation meeting, information packets, and follow-up workshops.

The Initial Orientation Meeting

As you respond to these topics, consider how you will disseminate the information you are providing.

The School District

• Organizational structure

• Personnel

• Methods of communication

• District goals

• The role of the school in fulfilling district goals

The School Mission and Philosophy

• How will the mission and philosophy statements be distributed?

• Where are the statements posted?

• What examples of the implementation of the mission and philosophy will be presented?

(Continued)

Chain of Command

- How will the organizational chart be distributed?

- What do new teachers need to know about the chain of command?

- When will the chain of command be important to first-year teachers' work?

Curriculum

- What aspects of the curriculum are important to new teachers?

- How will the curriculum be shared with new teachers?

- What part of the curriculum is the responsibility of new teachers?

School Calendar

- What do new teachers need to know about the school calendar?

- What special traditions or practices are embedded in the calendar?

Beginning of the Year Activities

- What special events occur at the beginning of the year?

- What information do new teachers need about these activities?

- What are first-year teachers' responsibilities related to these activities?

Required Meetings

- What meetings must new teachers attend?

- What are the purposes of the meetings?

- Who is responsible for the meetings?

Responsibilities

- What are the specific responsibilities of new teachers?

- Where are these responsibilities described?

(Continued)

Daily Schedules

- How are the daily schedules presented to first-year teachers?

- What do new teachers need to know about the schedules?

School Routines and Procedures

- Where are the routines and procedures described for new teachers?

- What are the unique aspects of these routines and procedures that new teachers need to know?

Record Keeping

- What are new teachers' record-keeping responsibilities?

- What tools do new teachers need to meet their record-keeping responsibilities?

- Who will provide assistance and skills training to new teachers as the record-keeping tools are used?

- What are the record-keeping checkpoints throughout the school year?

Fiscal Policies

- Which fiscal issues pertain to new teachers?

- Which fiscal issues are the teachers' responsibility?

Discipline Policy and Procedures

- What are the school's discipline policies and procedures?

- How are the policies and procedures enforced?

- Who is responsible for the various aspects of the policies and procedures?

- What are the expectations for teachers in the implementation and enforcement of discipline policies and procedures?

THE INFORMATION PACKET

To avoid burdening new teachers with information overload at the initial orientation meeting, provide them with a packet of printed information at the conclusion of the meeting. Suggest that participants read the information, save it for reference, and be prepared to ask questions at the next orientation session.

The Information Packet

Consider the following list of topics. Indicate the topics that are included in your information packet. (Check all that apply.)

Topics	✓
School mission and philosophy	
Chain of command (organization chart)	
Curriculum	
School calendar	
Beginning of the year activities calendar	
Required meetings	
Responsibilities	
Daily schedules	
School routines and procedures	
Record-keeping procedures	
Fiscal policies	
Discipline policy and procedures	

FOLLOW-UP ORIENTATION MEETINGS

Follow-up orientation meetings may include the topics that follow.

Meeting Topics

Information About the Student Body and Community

- What demographic information is available?

- Where is it located?

- How will it be presented?

- Who will present it?

Embracing Diversity

- What information do teachers need to have about the diversity issues they will encounter?

- Who will make the diversity presentations?

- What resources do teachers need to understand and work in a school with a diverse student population?

Basic School Routines and Procedures

- What questions do teachers have about routines and procedures?

(Continued)

Grading Policies

- What are the school's grading policies?

- How are these policies communicated to the students?

- How are these policies communicated to the parents?

Record Keeping

- What additional aspects of record keeping do first-year teachers need to understand?

- What questions do first-year teachers have about record keeping?

The School's Calendar

- What questions do teachers have about the calendar?

Beginning of School Activities

- What questions do teachers have about the beginning of school activities?

The School's Discipline Policy

- What questions or concerns do teachers have about the discipline policy?

SEMINARS

The topics of seminars, held throughout the year, should be derived from the needs of the new teachers. Typical concerns of new teachers include classroom management, differentiating instruction, inclusion, teaching English learners, assessment, and conferencing with parents.

THE PRINCIPAL'S ROLE IN ORIENTATION

The principal should be the leader in coordinating induction efforts, welcoming the new teachers, and presenting a strong, unified program (Brock & Grady, 1998). The presence and involvement of the principal in induction activities assures new teachers that they are welcomed, valued, and supported. The principal's specific responsibilities include

- Welcoming the new teachers
- Coordinating activities
- Involving the school personnel
- Sharing goals and expectations
- Limiting new teachers to realistic goals, assignments, and duties
- Scheduling time for induction activities
- Interacting with the new teachers

Since the principal is the formal leader of the school, the person who establishes expectations and who may evaluate them, new teachers will be listening and watching to determine the principal's educational philosophy, goals, and expectations. Knowing that, in their eagerness, new teachers typically volunteer for too many duties, the principal needs to discuss the importance of realistic goals and expectations for the first year of teaching as well as shield newcomers from unrealistic teaching assignments and duties.

KEY IDEAS

The contact person is important to the success of the new teacher. Identifying this person as well as her or his specific roles and responsibilities are important steps in the orientation process.

Planning orientation meetings requires attention to topics, sequencing, and pacing of information dissemination. Providing teachers with information packets reinforces the information provided during the orientation meetings.

7

The Mentorship Program

Although a successful orientation sets the stage for the induction process, many challenging weeks and months lie ahead. To provide ongoing assistance, many schools include mentors in their teacher induction program. Qualified and experienced teachers with a desire to work with new teachers are trained and assigned to assist one or more new teachers throughout the induction period.

THE REWARDS

A mentorship program during a teacher's first year can contribute to a satisfying and productive year for both the new teacher and the new teacher's students. In addition, mentored teachers tend to remain longer in their positions, develop self-reliance more quickly, and need less remediation (Portner, 2001).

Teachers who serve as mentors reap benefits in terms of personal renewal and professional growth (Moir, 2003). In addition, many mentors are offered some form of compensation, such as additional salary, release from teaching duties, university tuition waivers, or funding for conference travel.

The school and, most important, the students benefit from a network of highly skilled and enthusiastic teachers. Teacher isolation is replaced with collegiality.

DEVELOPING A MENTOR PROGRAM

The first steps in beginning a teacher-mentor program include performing a needs assessment to establish a program rationale and developing a desired standard for teaching performance. National, state, and district standards of professional practice and Charlotte Danielson's *Frameworks for Teaching* (1996) are commonly used performance benchmarks. Goals should be closely linked with student achievement and tailored to the school's setting and needs. A list of mentorship program goals includes the following:

- Retaining promising new teachers
- Improving the teaching performance of the new teachers
- Promoting the personal and professional well-being of new teachers
- Transmitting the culture of the school and teaching profession
- Developing leaders among the experienced faculty
- Promoting a network of collegiality among teachers
- Encouraging new teachers to share their ideas and expertise (Moir, 2003)
- Meeting district or state mandates

Mentorship Goals

State your commitment to each of the following goals. Describe specific actions you will take to achieve these goals.

Retaining promising new teachers

Commitment:

Action:

Improving the teaching performance of new teachers

Commitment:

Action:

Promoting the personal and professional well-being of new teachers

Commitment:

Action:

Transmitting the culture of the school and teaching profession

Commitment:

Action:

Developing leaders among the experienced faculty

Commitment:

Action:

Promoting a network of collegiality among teachers

Commitment:

Action:

Meeting district or state mandates

Commitment:

Action:

THE REQUIREMENTS FOR A MENTOR

Mentors should be experienced and excellent teachers who are able to plan and implement organized and academically stimulating lessons and have certification appropriate to the beginning teacher's assignment. Unless mentors are teachers of exceptional quality, they may perpetuate traditional teaching practices that are undesirable (Ganser, 2002; Jonson, 2002; Portner, 2001). Prerequisite areas for mentors are

- A positive and professional attitude
- A reputation as a highly skilled teacher
- The ability to communicate, interact, and work with a variety of people
- An understanding of child and adult learning theories
- The ability to define and solve problems
- Knowledge of assessment and evaluation
- Knowledge of the school's community and students
- Knowledge of school policies, procedures, curriculum, and resources
- A commitment to continued professional development

MATCHING NEW TEACHERS WITH MENTORS

Making the proper match between a new teacher and mentor is the first step in establishing a trusting mentoring relationship. To obtain effective matches, the following variables should be considered:

- Needs
- Grade level(s)
- Subjects
- Classroom proximity
- Ages and gender(s)
- Differences
- Enthusiasm for the mentoring program
- Teaching philosophies
- Interests

Matching New Teachers With Mentors

What priorities will be used to match new teachers with mentors? Indicate the priority ranking for each of the following considerations.

Considerations	Priority Rank
Informal meeting to determine needs	
Grade level(s)	
Subjects	
Classroom proximity	
Ages and gender	
Differences	
Enthusiasm for the mentoring program	
Teaching philosophies	
Interests	

THE MENTORING PROCESS

Mentoring programs that include structure and mutual understanding of mentor and mentee roles have a better basis of success (Kajs et al., 2003). In fact, one of the major causes of mentorship program failure is a lack of understanding of roles and a lack of procedural structure. New teachers who experienced failed mentoring relationships reported that mentoring processes were unfocused and irregular, and that they did not know the extent of the mentors' role. Some new teachers reported feeling like "bothers" to mentors who, instead of relying on regularly scheduled meetings, suggested that they ask for help whenever they need it (Brock & Grady, 2001).

The Mentoring Relationship

To maximize program effectiveness, the roles and responsibilities of mentors and mentees need to be identified. Use the questions below to more precisely define the mentoring relationship.

What are the mentor's roles and responsibilities?

What are the mentee's responsibilities?

What are the goals of the mentoring relationship?

What can the mentee expect from the mentor?

What are the anticipated benefits of the mentoring relationship for the mentor?

Structure for a mentoring program should include the following:

- Mentoring guidelines of month-by-month activities that correspond with events on the school's calendar (Jonson, 2002)
- Regularly scheduled meetings as well as spontaneous meetings
- Periodic assessments of new teachers' needs
- The development of action plans to focus interactions and goal attainment (Jonson, 2002)

Ideally, the mentoring process begins shortly after contract signing. If possible, the mentor should be the initial contact person or, at least, a member of the team that welcomes the new teacher and facilitates the transition process. Mentors should be available before school begins to answer questions and assist with classroom arrangements, securing materials, establishing classroom management procedures, and preparing lessons for the opening days. As the year progresses, mentoring can take a variety of forms, including teaching demonstrations, observations and feedback, direct assistance, suggestions, and emotional support.

Suggested responsibilities for mentors include

- Explaining school policies and procedures
- Answering questions
- Meeting regularly with the new teacher
- Demonstrating teaching methods
- Arranging peer observations
- Problem solving with the new teacher
- Sharing knowledge of teaching methods and materials
- Encouraging reflection about practice

Effective mentors listen, encourage, provide feedback, offer suggestions, share their time and experience, and model quality teaching.

The following exercises focus on the roles and responsibilities of mentors.

Mentors' Roles and Responsibilities

What will be the mentor's roles and responsibilities? (Check all that apply.)

Roles and Responsibilities	✓
Demonstrating teaching	
Arranging for peer observations	
Meeting regularly (daily, weekly) with mentee	
Answering questions	
Observing mentee's classroom	
Providing feedback after observations	
Providing direct assistance with problems	
Offering suggestions and new ideas	
Assisting with socialization	
Facilitating the development of the mentee's teaching network	

Mentors' Tasks

Does the mentor take responsibility for the following tasks? (Check all that apply.)

Tasks	✓
Explaining school procedures	
Explaining school culture and traditions	
Arranging opportunities for new teachers to observe other teachers	
Demonstrating and modeling teaching and classroom management strategies	
Problem solving to resolve curriculum, planning, time management, and discipline problems	
Sharing knowledge of teaching methods and use of materials	
Engaging teachers in reflection about their practice	

Mentors' Activities

When does each of these activities occur? Who is responsible for coordinating each of these activities? Respond to each of these questions in the space provided.

Mentor selection

When:

Who:

Mentor assignment

When:

Who:

Orientation sessions

When:

Who:

Meeting with mentors

When:

Who:

Meeting with principals

When:

Who:

Observations of teaching

When:

Who:

Formal meetings with teachers

When:

Who:

Informal meetings with teachers

When:

Who:

Interviews with first-year teachers

When:

(Continued)

Who:

Seminars

When:

Who:

Seminar evaluations

When:

Who:

Year-end evaluations

When:

Who:

MENTOR TRAINING

Successful mentor programs rely on mentors who know their roles and have the training and skills to fulfill those roles. Effective mentors require training, need opportunities to share experiences with colleagues, and need feedback from supervisors and novices (Ganser, 2003). When mentor programs fail, one source of the failure is a lack of training.

Content

The goals of the mentor program determine the content of the training and serve as the basis for mentor evaluation. Mentors identify new teachers' needs, assess their practice, and help them plan improvement that aligns with professional standards. Mentors routinely guide new teachers through reflections that evaluate the effectiveness of their teaching practices on student learning to evaluate how well teaching practices lead to student learning.

Mentors require a thorough knowledge of their school's policies, procedures, curriculum, and resources, as well as the subject and developmental levels of students they teach. In addition, mentors require an understanding of the kinds of problems that new teachers experience and the ability to adjust their mentoring role to meet changing needs as their mentee develops professionally (Kajs et al., 2003). Training in diagnosing problems, classroom observation, conferencing, and androgogy are highly desirable.

Diagnosing Needs

Mentoring is more effective when it is tailored to the needs of individual teachers. Individualizing assistance requires knowledge of the nature of a new teacher's problem. Usually, new teachers are eager to share their problems and concerns with their mentor. However, some novices may not have the ability to accurately identify and name the source of their problems. Other novices may be reluctant to share problems. Thus, mentors may need to use a combination of strategies to provide an accurate diagnosis. Diagnostic strategies that are useful to mentors include

- Listening to the new teacher's questions
- Employing questioning strategies
- Observing the new teacher
- Using assessment tools, like written surveys or personal interviews, that include questions on topics such as
  - School policies and procedures
  - Classroom organization
  - Teaching strategies

- Planning strategies
- Time management
- Classroom management
- Disciplinary measures
- Emotional support

Classroom Observation Skills

Classroom observations should occur regularly and be planned in advance by the mentor and the new teacher. Classroom observations afford new teachers the opportunity to obtain objective feedback on their teaching and to receive coaching relevant to their areas of concern. Mentors should be trained in classroom observation techniques, such as preconferencing, data collection strategies, and postconferencing.

Conferencing Skills

Conferencing techniques should be varied according to the new teachers' skill levels and motivation (Glickman et al., 2004). Each of the following three techniques requires knowledge of a distinct set of skills that should be part of a mentor's training:

- *Nondirective conferencing* is used with a new teacher who is highly motivated and has the ability to identify and solve problems. The function of the mentor is that of facilitator who guides the discovery process.
- *Collaborative conferencing* is used when the new teacher has some ideas but needs additional suggestions and advice. Mentor and new teacher engage in mutual problem analysis, brainstorming, and problem solving. They agree on a chosen solution and action plan.
- *Directive conferencing* is used when the new teacher does not have adequate skills for problem identification, problem analysis, or formulation of an effective solution. The mentor presents the problem and provides a solution and action plan for the new teacher (Glickman et al., 2004).

Androgogy

Although the individuals selected as mentors may be exceptional teachers, they may still have much to learn about mentoring adults, especially adult peers, which is considerably different from teaching children. Using an androgogical model, or learner-centered approach, usually yields the best results. Knowles's (1980) model follows:

- Adults prefer to be self-directing.
- Adults have a wealth of experience to augment learning.

- Adults are motivated to learn by a need to know or do something, which is problem-centered rather than subject-centered learning.
- Adults are motivated to learn due to internal or intrinsic factors rather than external or extrinsic forces.

Based on these assumptions, a logical choice of mentoring model is one that involves collaborative learning. Exceptions do exist, however, when situational variables intervene and the model doesn't work for a particular teacher. For instance, a new teacher who does not have the requisite skills or knowledge to be self-directed or collaborative may need more direction and support from the mentor. The learner's level of information, experience, and competence are key factors in determining the level of direct instruction and support that is required.

Mentors' Training

Consider the knowledge and skills you expect mentors to possess, individuals available to provide the training, and the time frame in which the training will occur. Check the desired knowledge and skills and identify the people who will provide the training and the time frame when it will occur.

✓	Desired Mentor Knowledge and Skills	Person With Knowledge or Skill	Time Frame for Training
	Understanding of adult learning		
	Knowledge of mentor roles		
	Active listening skills		
	Classroom observation skills		
	Skill in providing feedback		
	Direct assistance skills		
	Skill in providing suggestions		

PROFESSIONAL DEVELOPMENT FOR MENTORS

Being a mentor is a challenging responsibility, one that entails long hours, hard work, and occasional frustration.

Pitfalls can include

- Mentees who are reluctant, even resistant, to a mentor's assistance
- Mentees with problems beyond the mentor's expertise
- Becoming overextended, especially when a mentor has full-time teaching responsibilities
- Experiencing confusion and anxiety when expectations are unclear
- Becoming overly involved in the mentee's problems

Problems, confusion, and fatigue are avoidable through the use of professional growth opportunities designed specifically for mentors. Opportunities to interact, share information, acquire new skills, and obtain information on performance will provide enrichment and enable mentors to avoid potential pitfalls (Jonson, 2002).

How will your program support the professional development of mentors?

Professional Development Activities for Mentors

Consider the following questions:

1. How often will mentors meet as a group?

2. Who will facilitate the group meetings?

3. Who will evaluate mentors?

4. What sequence of topics will be addressed at the meetings?

5. What professional development opportunities will be offered to mentors (conference attendance, special skills workshops)?

6. How will mentors be evaluated?

7. What rewards and/or benefits will mentors receive?

8. What special recognition will mentors receive?

ACCOUNTABILITY

An accountability process will ensure regular meetings between and observations involving mentors and new teachers. The process might include indicators of mentor and new teacher activities, such as a log of meetings and classroom observations dates, and periodic formal reports from new teacher and mentor that summarize activities (Kajs et al., 2003).

A formal evaluation of the mentor program is necessary to ensure that program goals are met (Portner, 2001). Evaluation methods might include interviews and surveys of new teachers, individual learning plans, portfolios or other work products, student achievement data, and new teacher retention rates (Dexter, Berube, Moore, & Klopfenstein, 2005).

KEY IDEAS

The mentorship program provides many rewards to participants. The program needs to be based on clearly defined goals. Once goals are identified, expectations for mentors are established. Matching new teachers with mentors should be based on considerations such as grade level, age, subject area, gender, philosophy, and interests. The mentoring program needs to be structured based on roles, responsibilities, a calendar, and planned activities.

8

Classroom Management

Classroom management issues are a major concern for new teachers, a frequent source of problems, and the number one reason these teachers leave the profession. Left unchecked, chronic discipline problems can undermine the success of a talented teacher.

Effective classroom management, combined with strong teaching strategies, meaningful content, and a sound organizational structure form the ingredients necessary for productive teaching and learning (Larrivee, 2005). An orderly classroom makes it possible for learning to occur.

PROBLEM SOURCES

Various factors contribute to new teachers' discipline problems.

- Teachers beginning their careers have had limited exposure to classroom management techniques during preservice preparation. Training may have been limited to introducing teachers to theoretical approaches to classroom management, with suggestions for handling misbehavior (Jones & Jones, 1998).
- New teacher experiences with classroom management and discipline usually consist of a semester or two of student teaching under the watchful eyes of a supervisor. New teachers may begin their first assignment unaware of the diversity of student transgressions they will encounter.
- Individual schools have different expectations for classroom management and disciplinary measures.
- New teachers may be unfamiliar with the cultural, linguistic, or academic diversity in the school setting (Larrivee, 2005). Cultural or language differences may be the source of perceived misbehaviors.

DECREASING DISCIPLINE PROBLEMS

Although there is no magic prevention or cure for discipline problems, induction programs that incorporate the following measures can decrease the frequency of problems and improve the likelihood of new teachers' success:

- School discipline policies and procedures that are enforced consistently
- An orientation for new teachers on school discipline policies and procedures
- Seminars for new teachers on classroom management, such as causes of behavior problems, preventative measures, and how to respond to student misbehavior
- Direct assistance to new teachers who experience specific discipline problems

THE SCHOOL AND ITS LEADERSHIP

The teacher's ability to maintain classroom discipline is linked to the discipline level of the school. The school, as an institution, contributes to students' levels of motivation and academic self-concept, both of which directly influence student behavior (Larivee, 2005; Oliva & Pawlas, 2004).

Answers to the following questions can be helpful in determining if a school is student-friendly:

1. Do adults show respect for students?
2. Do adults demonstrate a caring attitude?
3. Is student pride in achievement nurtured?
4. Is the school bright and cheerful?
5. Is student work displayed?
6. Is the curriculum relevant to students' experiences?
7. Is self-expression fostered?
8. Is a spirit of teamwork encouraged? (Sergiovanni & Starratt, 2002)

Schools that are not student-friendly view students as untrustworthy adversaries. Students are coerced, intimidated, and badgered into learning. The climate is one of control, passive conformity, and automatic obedience underscored by the threat of punishment (Sergiovanni & Starratt, 2002).

Discipline problems in schools include a range aptly described by Oliva and Pawlas (2004) as "from the trivial to the terrifying and from the casual to the criminal" (p. 168). Student misbehavior can range from minor class disruptions to acts of physical violence. Although some schools experience only minimal or minor discipline problems, other schools experience frequent misbehavior that threatens the safety of those in the school. Increases in school violence, drug use, and other serious offenses should make rigorous preventative measures a necessity for every school.

Factors such as culture, climate, morale, curriculum, and building upkeep contribute to the school's disciplinary level (Oliva & Pawlas, 2004). Additional contributing factors include the principal's expectations for student behavior, adherence to school discipline policy and procedures, and support of teachers' disciplinary actions. The principal plays an important role in establishing the level of school discipline as well as assisting new teachers in preventing and solving classroom discipline problems.

FACTORS THAT CONTRIBUTE TO A SCHOOL'S DISCIPLINARY LEVEL

These factors include the school's

- Culture
- Morale

- Climate
- Curriculum
- Cleanliness and upkeep
- Clear discipline policies and procedures
- Consistent adherence to discipline policies and procedures

As important to school discipline are the principal's

- Expectations for behavior
- Enforcement of discipline policy and procedures
- Support of teachers' disciplinary decisions

Principals of schools with effective discipline

- Are aware of the role of culture, climate, and morale in school discipline
- Strive to maintain a curriculum that is relevant to student's needs
- Ensure that the building and grounds are kept clean and well maintained
- Adhere to established school discipline policies and procedures
- Maintain and share high expectations for student behavior
- Make safety for students and personnel a priority
- Are visible and present throughout the school
- Handle serious disciplinary infractions, such as violence toward people and destruction of property, to ensure a safe teaching environment
- Maintain a consistent policy for student referrals to the office
- Support teachers' disciplinary decisions
- Provide beginning teacher seminars on the relationship between learning and the cultural, linguistic, and academic diversity of the students
- Provide beginning teacher seminars on classroom management
- Provide beginning teacher seminars on the school's discipline policy and appropriate responses to student behavior
- Provide new teacher seminars on interacting and conferencing with parents
- Provide new teachers with direct assistance when needed

The exercises that follow examine the school in terms of the principal's role and views of discipline and factors associated with orderly schools.

The Principal's Role in Discipline

Consider the following questions regarding the principal's role in discipline and determine the improvements that should occur in your school.

Is the school a safe place to teach?
What improvements should be made?

Are you consistent in disciplinary measures?
What improvements should be made?

Are you visible in all corners of the school and campus?
What improvements should be made?

What are your expectations for student behavior?

What improvements should be made?

(Continued)

Do teachers know the expectations for student behavior?
What improvements should be made?

What are your expectations for teacher responses to student misbehavior?

What improvements should be made?

Do teachers know your expectations of them?
What improvements should be made?

Do you support teachers' disciplinary decisions?
What improvements should be made?

What training related to discipline do you provide for new teachers?
What improvements should be made?

DEFINITIONS OF DISCIPLINE

Discipline is a widely used term that can mean different things to different people. The word can signify the order maintained in a classroom, the means employed to establish that order, the method used to punish offenders who destroy order, and/or the control imposed on oneself, that is, self-discipline (Oliva & Pawlas, 2004).

Views of Discipline

Are these definitions of discipline understood in your school? (Check all that apply.)

Definitions	✓
The degree of order maintained in the classroom. This is discipline we have.	
The means employed to establish, maintain, or restore order in the classroom. This is discipline we use.	
The specific means we use to punish offenders. In this sense, discipline is the punishment we inflict.	
The means we use to develop self-discipline or self-control. This is the discipline we live.	

SCHOOLS WITH GOOD DISCIPLINE

The Phi Delta Kappa Commission on Discipline identified eight factors associated with schools with good discipline (Wayson, DeVoss, Kaeser, Lasley, Pinnell, & Phi Delta Kappa Commission on Discipline, 1982).

Schools With Good Discipline

Consider how each of these factors manifests itself in your school:

The Way People in a School Work Together to Solve Problems

Describe how your staff work together to solve problems.

The Way Authority and Status Are Allocated and Symbolized in the School

Who has authority in the school?

Who has status in the school?

What are the symbols of authority in the school?

What are the symbols of status in the school?

The Degree to Which Students Feel They Belong to the School and Feel It Serves Them

What evidence indicates students feel they belong to the school?

How are students encouraged to feel part of the school?

What evidence indicates students feel the school serves them?

(Continued)

How does the school serve the students?

The Way Rules Are Developed, Communicated, and Enforced

How are rules developed, communicated, and enforced in the school?

The Ways of Dealing With Personal Problems of Students and Staff

How do you deal with the personal problems of students?

How do you deal with the personal problems of staff?

What resources are available to deal with these problems?

The Ways in Which the Physical Facilities and the
Organizational Structure of the School Reinforce Educational Goals

How do the school's physical facilities reinforce school goals?

How does the organizational structure of the school reinforce school goals?

The Relationship Among the School, the Community, and the Homes Served

How is the school's relationship with the community nurtured?

The Quality of the Curriculum and Instructional Practices

How is the quality of the curriculum measured?

How are excellent instructional practices maintained?

What activities are available to teachers to improve instructional practices?

HELPING NEW TEACHERS WITH DISCIPLINE

In addition to needing a strong, positive disciplinary climate in the school, new teachers also require assistance in establishing classroom environments conducive to student leaning. An induction program including the following components can be beneficial.

1. Defining a discipline problem

2. Discussing causes of behavior problems

3. Providing skills and strategies for preventing discipline problems

4. Suggesting corrective measures for transgressions (Bear, 2005; Jones & Jones, 1998; Levin & Nolan, 2004; Oliva & Pawlas, 2004)

In spite of negative media attention, most school behavior problems do not involve violence or criminal activity. Instead, the most frustrating and plaguing disciplinary problem for new teachers usually involves dealing with student behavior that disrupts the learning environment. However, what types of student behaviors constitute disruptive behavior is subject to debate (Levin & Nolan, 2004). Thus, a discussion of what constitutes a discipline problem is a good place to begin.

Defining a Discipline Problem

According to Levin and Nolan (2004), understanding what is considered a discipline problem is fundamental to the development of classroom rules, identification of misbehaviors that occur, and development of intervention strategies for behavior change. Levine and Nolan (2004) further recommend using a comprehensive definition that defines a discipline problem as any behavior that disrupts the teaching act, is psychologically or physically unsafe, or is destructive. New teachers struggle to identify the importance of a discipline problem. They have difficulty differentiating which problems are serious and require attention and which ones should be ignored. Some new teachers wear themselves out trying to attend to every minor problem that occurs, while others ignore too many misbehaviors.

CAUSES OF BEHAVIOR PROBLEMS

Struggling day after day with disrespectful and disruptive students is frustrating and discouraging. New teachers want to know how to eliminate student disruption from their classrooms so they can teach more effectively. Examining the underlying sources of student misbehavior is the first step.

Children's behaviors are motivated and chosen according to what they want and need (Glasser, 1998). Consequently, children behave better and learn more effectively when their basic personal and psychological needs are satisfied. Outside influences on behavior include the child's peer group, the teacher, the school climate, the child's home and neighborhood, and societal conditions (Oliva & Pawlas, 2004; Sergiovanni & Starrat, 2002). Teachers who understand and respond to student needs and understand the impact of outside influences will have fewer problems with discipline.

Some teachers are quick to place blame on outside forces and absolve themselves from taking corrective action. Outside influences, however, do not absolve teachers from their responsibility. Although teachers do not have control of a student's environment, they do have control of their classrooms. Rather than placing blame, a better choice is adapting the learning environment to meet the needs of the student (Jones & Jones, 1998).

The key to effective discipline is structuring the learning environment to meet student needs. To do so, teachers need to understand how the following factors contribute to student behavior.

Personal Issues

Personal factors may reveal sources of discipline problems as well as suggest solutions for improving behavior, such as working with parents to address a physical or health problem, adapting teaching methods to the child's stage of growth and development or mental ability, and attempting to raise a child's self-concept. Personal factors to consider include the child's

- Physical problems—such as hearing and vision difficulties
- General health—such as nutrition, rest, and presence of disease
- Stage of growth and development—the child's ability to sit still, listen, understand abstract concepts, and solve problems
- Mental ability—the level of work that yields frustration, dissatisfaction, or boredom
- Academic self-concept—the child's perception of self (Oliva & Pawlas, 2004)
- Sense of self-efficacy
- Sense of control over destiny
- Motivation to learn—the relative importance to the child of good grades, promotion, diploma, potential job or street smarts, and luck (Sergiovanni & Starratt, 2002).
- Sense of belonging (Glasser, 1998)

Peer Group Pressure

A student's behavior may be influenced by the student's peer group. Most students have a group of friends inside and outside the school. This group of peers can play a powerful role in student behavior, especially during teenage years. In schools in which youth gangs are prevalent, peer pressure is a particularly difficult competitor. The solution involves creating a classroom environment in which the student finds satisfaction and a sense of identity and belonging. Teachers should consider the impact of the following groups:

- Friends inside and outside school
- Youth gangs (Oliva & Pawlas, 2004)

Teachers' Behaviors

The teacher's attitude toward students and method of instruction contribute to classroom climate. Discipline problems are more likely when teachers are uncaring and disrespectful toward students or use teaching methods and content that are inappropriate for the learner. New teachers who are unfamiliar with students' culture and inexperienced in teaching pedagogy are particularly vulnerable to these problems.

Teachers with the following attributes and teaching methods generally have fewer discipline problems:

- Attitude
  - Genuine interest in students
  - Satisfaction with their job and school
  - Respect for students and parents
  - Appreciation of students' cultures
  - A sense of humor (Oliva & Pawlas, 2004)

- Instructional methods
  - Appropriate objectives
  - Good planning
  - Effective presentation
  - Suitable materials
  - Adequate evaluation
  - Adequate feedback (Oliva & Pawlas, 2004)

- Curriculum
  - Relevant to students' lives
  - With an appropriate level of difficulty (Kauffman, Mostert, Trent, & Hallahan, 2002)

Students' Needs

Indicate which of these needs are being met at your school. (Check all that apply.)

Considerations	✓
All children need to feel and believe that they are capable and successful.	
All children need to realize that they are able to influence people and events.	
All children need to practice helping others through their own generosity.	
All children need to experience fun and stimulation.	
All children need to feel they belong.	

PREVENTING DISCIPLINE PROBLEMS

Some teachers do not encounter discipline problems because they know how to prevent them. Preventing discipline problems is preferable to managing discipline problems. Teachers known for their mastery of preventative discipline demonstrate the following skills and attributes:

- A genuine, caring attitude toward students
- A willingness to work with parents
- A positive relationship with each student
- An understanding of each student's needs
- Emotional control
- High expectations for student learning
- The ability to foster positive peer relationships
- Confidence in their teaching ability
- A willingness and ability to adapt teaching style to student needs

- A well-organized classroom
- Purposeful lesson planning
- Stimulating, well-planned lessons that engage students in meaningful tasks
- A sense of humor
- The use of appropriate models of discipline
- Appropriate classroom rules

Although some teachers may have a natural gift for managing classrooms, all teachers can improve their discipline by learning preventative skills, such as

- Establishing classroom rules and procedures
- Creating a positive physical climate
- Providing a positive academic climate
- Maintaining order
- Establishing high expectations for student success
- Planning and delivering stimulating lessons

New teachers will benefit from sessions that include information and suggestions on preventative techniques. Principals should also provide opportunities for discussion, role-playing, and observations of veteran teachers who effectively employ the techniques. Suggestions for new teacher induction on preventative discipline include

1. Informative sessions on strategies to prevent discipline problems

2. Observation of teachers using exemplary classroom discipline followed by discussion of preventative discipline strategies

3. Peer observation of the new teacher's classroom followed by discussion of preventative discipline strategies

4. Question and answer sessions on the topic of preventative discipline

5. Direct assistance with specific discipline problems

Topics for seminars on preventative discipline might include

- Establishing positive teacher-student relationships
- Interacting with parents
- Identifying student needs
- Understanding cultural differences
- Weighing importance of student misbehavior
- Expectancy theory and student learning
- Fostering classroom peer relationships

- Teaching and learning styles
- Classroom organization
- Lesson planning
- Lesson delivery
- Differentiating instruction
- Creating stimulating and appropriate lessons
- Motivating students
- Models of discipline
- Developing classroom behavior standards
- Assessing the classroom environment

Physical Aspects of the Classroom

How the desks and other classroom furniture are arranged can either enhance or deter good instruction and classroom management. New teachers need to plan how they will use several aspects of physical space, including how they will arrange classroom furniture, use walls and bulletin board space, and store and file materials (Burden & Cooper, 2004). The arrangement of student desks should include walkways that afford the teacher easy access to students (Jones, 2001) and enable students to see all instructional areas.

Classrooms should appear welcoming, clean, and aesthetically pleasing. Bulletin boards should be used to display student work and to enhance instruction.

Classroom Rules

Students who understand teacher expectations and school rules are more likely to behave appropriately. New teachers should develop a short and simple list of classroom rules, explain and model them, post them in the classroom, and apply them consistently and fairly.

Classroom Rules

Are the classroom rules evident in the school and in each classroom? Rules should be restricted to five simple questions.

Questions for Students	✓
1. Are you respecting others' rights to learn?	
2. Are you respecting others' rights not to be hurt physically or by put-downs?	
3. Are you respecting others' rights to their personal property?	
4. Are you helping others?	
5. Are you making others feel good by giving compliments or by inviting them to join you in some activity?	

Classroom Routines and Procedures

Teachers who establish routines to begin and end class and procedures to accomplish specific tasks have fewer discipline problems (Burden & Cooper, 2004). New teachers should plan to have work on the board when students enter the room and have a routine for ending class. Classrooms operate more smoothly when teachers have identified procedures for the following tasks:

- Seating students on the first day
- Distributing textbooks on the first day
- Sharpening pencils
- Turning in work
- Completing make-up work
- Using the restroom
- Distributing materials
- Putting away supplies

- Retrieving forgotten items from lockers
- Signaling the teacher for assistance
- Borrowing pencils and materials

Communication With Parents

Communication between teacher and parents should be established by a letter of introduction or phone call before the first day of school, with a plan for ongoing contacts throughout the school year.

Lesson Plans for the First Days

Lessons during the first few days should be motivating, have a high student success rate, and focus on whole group instruction. Using whole group instruction makes it easier to monitor behavior, reinforce positive behavior, and stop inappropriate behaviors. Teachers should be visible, moving around the classroom, should be available to students, and should appear confident and in charge (Burden & Cooper, 2004).

RESPONDING TO MISBEHAVIOR

New teachers typically receive different levels of preparation for handling student behavior problems. Some will be well prepared, while others will struggle due to inadequate training.

New teachers who are inadequately trained model their responses to student misbehavior on personal experiences rather than on theories and practices learned in preparation programs. They attribute misbehavior to student attitudes. Punitive measures, rather than instructional approaches, are common responses. Current theory suggests that behavior problems should be treated with instruction in the same way that academic problems are treated. Students who misbehave should receive assistance in developing alternative responses (Kauffman et al., 2002).

Induction programs can assist new teachers in learning current theories, broadening their views, and building a repertoire of strategies to handle student misbehaviors. Suggested induction program topics include

- School policy and procedures for handling student misbehavior
- Due process
- A comparison of punitive and instructional approaches to misbehavior
- Research on the effects of control and punishment
- Maintaining self-control
- Handling minor disruptions
- Handling major disruptions
- Dealing with persistent misbehavior

- Responding to noncompliant or defiant behavior
- De-escalating emotional behavior
- Handling violent student behavior
- Using problem solving to redirect behavior
- Mediating student conflicts
- Classroom problem solving (Jones & Jones, 1998)
- The referral process for unremitting problematic behavior
- The role of punishment (Oliva & Pawlas, 2004)

KEY IDEAS

Principals should determine new teachers' levels of training and experience with classroom management before school begins and provide assistance accordingly. Instructing teachers in the school's discipline policy and procedures, preventative discipline strategies, and measures to correct misbehavior will ensure a productive year.

9

Continuous Development

In spite of effective induction programs, many beginning teachers leave teaching with less than seven years of experience. Teachers who flourished during the induction years often flounder when support diminishes. They feel abandoned and without direction. Some leave the profession within a few years; others remain but never achieve their full teaching potential.

THE NEED FOR CONTINUOUS DEVELOPMENT

Induction is not an isolated program, but rather the first phase of a career-long professional development plan. The goal of induction programs is to address the concerns of teachers in the beginning stages of professional development. After the induction phase ends, however, a teacher's need for professional development continues. New teachers need to transition into a supportive program of continuous development. Unless teachers are assisted in making this transition, their development may cease prematurely. Teachers who encounter a professional void after the induction period often become frustrated, become disenchanted, leave the profession, or even worse, join the ranks of the mediocre.

STAGES OF DEVELOPMENT

Teachers experience several phases of development throughout their careers. Awareness of individual teachers' developmental levels and corresponding needs are important considerations when planning for their continuous learning. Steffy, Wolfe, Pasch, and Enz (2000) described a developmental continuum for teachers:

- Novice (preservice practicum experiences)
- Apprentice (early years; first independent teaching)
- Professional (growing in confidence; aware of efficacy of teaching)
- Expert (achievement of high standards of teaching; national certification level)
- Distinguished (gifted teacher; revered and consulted at state and national levels)
- Emeritus (lifetime achievement in the profession)

According to this developmental continuum, new teachers are at the apprentice stage. They are energetic and idealistic, yet overwhelmed and filled with self-doubt. Their attainment of the higher levels of growth requires involvement in continuous development.

LEVELS OF CONCERN

Equally important and related to teachers' stages of development is their level of concern. Categories of teachers' levels of concern include

- A focus on self or self-adequacy
- A focus on teaching tasks
- Concern for their impact on students
- A desire to contribute to the school community
- A desire to contribute to the teaching profession (Glickman et al., 2004)

During the first years of teaching, new teachers are idealistic and enthusiastic, but they may be overwhelmed by the enormity of daily preparation and teaching. Their immediate concern is maintaining classroom order, teaching today's classes, and finding time to prepare for tomorrow. Focused on daily survival, they have little time and energy for schoolwide issues and problems (Glickman et al., 2004). Although some newcomers are quick to develop confidence and gravitate toward advanced teaching practices, others fail to progress past the early survival strategies.

The first five years of teaching are the formative building years. During this critical period, new teachers experience the complexities of the classroom and begin to build confidence and competence in teaching practices (Zepeda, 1999). Continuing assistance enables new teachers to gain the confidence and skills that advance them past daily survival to concern for their impact on students and desire to contribute to the school and profession.

Understanding a new teacher's level of concern is the starting point in providing developmental assistance (Glickman et al., 2004). The following exercise addresses your experiences with teachers' levels of concern and how they impact their teaching.

Levels of Concern

From your work with first-year teachers, provide examples of teachers who had each of these concerns.

A focus on self or self-adequacy:

Teaching task concerns:

Concern for the impact on students:

A desire to contribute to the school community:

A desire to contribute to the teaching profession:

INCREASING CHALLENGES

Moving new teachers along a developmental continuum from survivor to self-directed professional requires continuing assistance. New teachers face more challenges than ever before. State reform initiates demand that teachers master new skills and change their practices and, in so doing, raise the educational level of all students. Meanwhile, the cultural, linguistic, and economic diversity of students in U.S. schools is growing (Hodgkinson, 2002), and an increasing number of students are English language learners (Lenhardt, 2000).

To meet these challenges and expectations, new teachers need to experience new techniques, test their ideas, and master approaches that serve student needs. They must become reflective practitioners in order to monitor and adjust their teaching to meet changing student needs. To do so, they require a continuous development plan that extends the learning initiated during induction.

PLANNING FOR CONTINUOUS DEVELOPMENT

The assumption of development programs is that all who work in the learning business must continue to learn. When development is delayed or inadequate, new teachers become discouraged, quit, or settle for mediocrity (Sargent, 2003). The most zealous and promising novices often become victims of burnout (Brock & Grady, 2000).

The purpose of staff development activities must be clearly stated and related to the central function of the school—that of improving student learning (DuFour, 1999b). To be effective, a development program must promote best professional practices while simultaneously responding to the mission of the school district, individual school goals, and individual teacher needs. Factors involved in development program decisions include faculty strengths and weaknesses, student needs, district goals, reform issues, state mandates, and available resources.

Although research in the 1980s heightened awareness and brought new knowledge and innovation to staff development, few school districts made radical program changes. Over two decades later, faculty development programs remain minimal or ineffective (Cochran-Smith & Lytle, 2001; Darling-Hammond & Sykes, 1999). Teachers continue to suffer through presentations and training sessions that are often unrelated to their teaching needs. It is no wonder teachers regard staff development as boring, unproductive, and a waste of time. They long for staff development that improves their teaching and the learning of their students.

USEFUL STRATEGIES

The following strategies can be useful in designing a development program (Ashby & Krug, 1998). Consider how you might incorporate the following strategies into a continuous development program:

Development Program Strategies

Strategy	Positive (+) and Negative (−) Aspects
1. Individually guided development	+ Adults learn best when they initiate and plan their learning − It's repetitious if several new teachers need the same information
2. Observation and assessment	+ Teachers receive feedback from the supervisor regarding their teaching − It's negatively associated with evaluation
3. Peer coaching	+ Teachers receive feedback regarding their teaching from a peer − It's a scheduling challenge and some teachers resist it
4. Solving school problem	+ Teachers study the issue and gather information − Teachers must be vested in the problem
5. Training	+ It promotes teachers' awareness and increases their knowledge − It assumes that the information provided is relevant and needed
6. Inquiry	+ Teachers study problems that emerge from practice − Maturity, experience, and knowledge of practice are required to formulate the questions

A MODEL FOR CONTINUOUS DEVELOPMENT

The basic assumptions about what constitutes an effective continuous development program are similar to those regarding an effective induction program. Although varying models of professional development exist (Drago-Severson, 2004; Fullan, 2000; Gordon, 2004; Steffy et al., 2000; Zepeda, 1999), many continuous development programs are

- Supported by the school or district leadership and financial resources
- Grounded in the needs of the individual learner
- Responsive to teachers as adult learners
- Linked to improved student learning
- Supported by a collegial learning environment
- Offered at times and locations accessible to teachers
- Evaluated regularly

Components of continuous development should include elements that facilitate new teacher transition from the induction phase to the continuous development phase. Novices need to replace dependence on mentor assistance with increasing self-reliance and problem-solving skills. In order for this transition to occur, opportunities for reflection and collaboration are essential. Enhancement of reflective thinking skills, initiated during induction, enables teachers to come up with a deeper analysis of problems and a wider repertoire of solutions. Collaboration with veteran faculty helps new teachers examine how teaching impacts student learning, exposes novices to new strategies, encourages teachers to share their ideas, and promotes teachers' self-confidence in analyzing and modifying teaching practices. DuFour (1999b) recommends the following strategies to maximize the effectiveness of collaboration:

- Build time for collaboration into the school day and year.
- Ensure that collaboration has a stated purpose and measurable performance goals.
- Make collaboration results oriented.

Since teachers learn best when they are seeking information and solutions relevant to their work issues, the success of a continuous development program is more likely if it is built on the principles of adult learning theory. The following model of continuous development is guided by principles of adult learning theory (Knowles, 1980). In this model, teachers are treated as professionals who are capable of identifying and pursuing professional growth needs. Reflective thinking and faculty collaboration are key elements. New teachers engage in collaborative learning activities with more experienced colleagues and in individually guided development activities with their supervisors. Large group presentations, seminars, courses, and other in-service sessions flow from teacher needs and the mission of the school or district. The role of the supervisor or principal is to monitor activities, provide resources, arrange presentations, and provide formative observations with feedback.

A MODEL FOR CONTINUOUS LEARNING

1. Individualized Development
   - Goal selection: The teacher selects a goal related to practice and in collaboration with the supervisor identifies a process of goal attainment
   - Measures of goal attainment: The teacher's self-evaluation, portfolio, and teaching demonstration with observation and feedback by the supervisor

2. Group Inquiry
   - Purpose: Collaborative learning on a topic related to improvement of teaching
   - Topic of study: A topic, determined by group consensus, that is relevant to teaching practice and improved student learning
   - Composition: Between five and ten teachers grouped by the principal to reflect similarities in grade levels or subject areas but diversity in age, experience, gender, and culture
   - Leadership: The group leader and recorder are selected by the principal
   - Duration: Weekly meetings for one semester
   - Role of the principal: Facilitator, monitor, procurer of resources
   - Evaluation: Each group member documents personal efforts and student outcomes

3. Large Group Learning
   - Reflective thinking: Teachers receive instruction and encouragement in the use of reflective thinking skills
   - Peer observations: Opportunities are provided for teachers to observe peers within and outside of the school district
   - Presentations, seminars, conferences: Topics and formats are selected in response to teacher need, school and district goals, and reform initiatives

4. Formative Observation and Feedback by the Supervisor
   - The supervisor observes each teacher and provides feedback about the teacher's progress toward the goal
   - The supervisor provides encouragement, assistance, recognition, and rewards

A Proposed Model for Continuous Development: Key Considerations

1. What are the components of the current development program?

2. How are new teachers currently transitioned from the induction phase to the continuous development phase?

3. What components do you propose for a revised development program?

THE PRINCIPAL'S ROLE IN DEVELOPMENT

The role of the principal or supervisor in a development program is that of leader and facilitator (Drago-Severson, 2004; DuFour, 1999a). In addition, principals who personally engage in professional development are more likely to motivate teachers to do so (Gordon, 2004). Although principals need to lead the effort, input from teachers who participate in the program is an essential factor in accurately identifying program needs. The involvement of teachers in the program design, content, and delivery links the program to student-teacher interactions and ensures a strong level of teacher commitment (Gordon, 2004).

The principal's role in teacher development includes the following responsibilities:

- To inspire teachers to improve their instructional practices
- To identify teachers' professional development needs through observations, surveys, conversations, and requests

- To facilitate the delivery of learning activities that will fulfill teachers' developmental needs
- To provide teachers with necessary resources, recognition, and rewards
- To establish an environment that supports collegiality and collaboration

CONDITIONS FOR CONTINUOUS PROFESSIONAL DEVELOPMENT

The quality of a school's learning environment is a major factor in the success of a development program. Learning is more apt to occur in environments with high levels of mutual trust, open communication, and collegiality (Drago-Severson, 2004). Little's (1982) study of the workplace conditions in six urban schools revealed that continuous professional development was most thoroughly achieved when the following conditions prevailed:

- Teachers engaged in frequent, continuous talk about teaching practice.
- Teachers frequently observed and provided with feedback about their teaching.
- Teachers designed, prepared, and evaluated teaching materials together.
- Teachers taught each other the art of teaching.

Conditions for Continuous Professional Development

Examine your school's learning environment. Which of the following conditions exist? (Check all that apply.)

Conditions of the Learning Environment	✓
Teachers engaging in frequent, continuous talk about teaching practice	
Teachers being frequently observed and provided with feedback about their teaching	
Teachers designing, preparing, and evaluating teaching materials together	
Teachers teaching each other the art of teaching	

Steps to Encourage Continuous Professional Development

What steps will you take to create conditions that contribute to continuous professional growth? For each of the following conditions, list what will be done to improve the school's learning environment.

Teachers engaging in frequent, continuous talk about teaching practice

Steps to improvement:

Teachers frequently being observed and provided feedback about their teaching

Steps to improvement:

Teachers designing, preparing, and evaluating teaching materials together

Steps to improvement:

Teachers teaching each other the art of teaching

Steps to improvement:

AN ENVIRONMENT FOR LEARNING

Continuous learning occurs best in environments where group members trust each other, exhibit mutual respect, and engage in open and honest, two-way communication (Pasch, Wolfe, Steffy, & Enz, 2000). Examine the environment in your school.

The Work Environment

Describe how each of the following is nurtured in your school.

Mutual respect of first-year teacher and mentor:

Collaboration among peers:

Trust within the staff:

Supportive peers and administration:

Openness and authenticity of expression:

Pleasurable learning experiences:

ESTABLISHING A CLIMATE OF COLLEGIALITY

A sense of collegiality exists in settings that foster continuous learning. Teachers share ideas, collaborate, and engage in meaningful discussions about teaching and learning. A sense of cooperation and mutual support exists. Teachers feel safe to try new ideas and take risks.

A climate of collegiality does not occur accidentally. Collegiality is fostered through the principal's actions, words, and modeling (Pasch et al., 2000).

Collegiality

For each of the following items, indicate what actions should be taken to promote collegiality.

Stating expectations for collegiality:

Collaborating with faculty in making school improvements:

Providing recognition, funding, materials, or space to teachers who collaborate:

Supporting teachers as they demonstrate collegial behaviors:

REFLECTIVE PRACTITIONERS

The ultimate goal of teacher development is increased student learning through improvements in teaching practice. Quality teaching is more apt to occur when teachers routinely engage in critical reflection and make adaptations in response to student needs.

New teachers require assistance to become reflective practitioners. Although some of them may have received training in reflection during preservice programs, they may need a "refresher" in order to refine the art of reflection. In addition, during preservice and induction new teachers may become overly reliant on suggestions of supervisors and mentors. As teachers progress in their careers, they need to learn how to analyze and solve their teaching problems and to trust their judgment.

Continuous development programs that include information and practice in the following areas can be helpful:

- Basic skills in reflection
- Guided practice in reflection
- Group practice in reflection
- Problem-solving strategies
- Understanding student needs
- Identifying student learning styles
- Identifying personal teaching style
- Differentiated teaching strategies
- Assessing student progress

Reflection should be encouraged in group as well as individual settings. Learning to reflect in a group setting encourages collaboration, serves to widen teachers' perspectives, and offers a reflective view of their work in the larger context of school and the teaching profession (Drago-Severson, 2004).

The goal of continuous development is to stimulate and improve the practices of new and veteran teachers. An effective development program can transition a new teacher from being a survivor to being someone prepared to embrace and negotiate the complexities of the teaching profession.

REFLECTIVE THINKING

Consider each of the following issues.

1. How will reflection skills be taught?

2. When will reflection skills be introduced?

3. What reflection skills will be taught?

4. How will the reflective practice sessions be arranged?

5. How will small groups of teachers be encouraged to engage in reflection?

6. How will teachers be encouraged to become interested in school-wide activities?

7. How will teachers be encouraged to become interested in the larger issues of the teaching profession?

8. What other development activities will be included in the process?

KEY IDEAS

The induction program is the first step in a career-long development program. Transition to a program of continuous development is necessary for the new teacher to achieve full potential. Without the provision of professional growth opportunities after induction, new teachers are more likely to leave the profession. Those who remain often fail to flourish and remain among the unmotivated and uninspired. The most effective continuous professional development occurs in supportive and collegial school environments under the leadership of a supportive principal.

10

The Induction Plan

The final step is developing a written induction plan based on the information that has been collected about the teachers and the school. The following format will serve as a guide.

The Written Induction Plan

Definitions of Key Terms

- What terms need to be defined?

- What are their definitions?

A Statement of Purpose

- What is the purpose of the induction program?

The Program Rationale

- What is the need for an induction program in the school?

- What are the goals of the induction program?

- Who will be responsible for accomplishing each of the goals?

- What is the timeline for accomplishing each goal?

- What steps will be taken to achieve the goals?

- What will be the indicators of the accomplishment of each goal?

- How will the induction program be presented to the stakeholders?

Responsibility for Goal Accomplishment

- Who will be responsible for each goal?

Resources

- What resources will be needed?

(Continued)

Orientation

- Describe the orientation process.

- Who is responsible for each aspect of the orientation process?

- What resources are needed for the orientation process?

- What is the timeline for the orientation process?

Mentors

- How will mentors be selected?

- How will mentors be trained?

The Workplace

- How will an environment supportive of the induction program be developed?
  - Goals:

  - Timelines:

  - Steps:

- How will a workplace supportive of ongoing professional development be created?
  - Goals:

  - Timelines:

  - Steps:

(Continued)

- How will the environment for student learning be improved?
  - Goals:

  - Timeline:

  - Steps:

- What resources will be needed to achieve these goals?

A Process for Program Evaluation

- How will the program be evaluated?

Resource A:
A Teacher Induction
Program Model

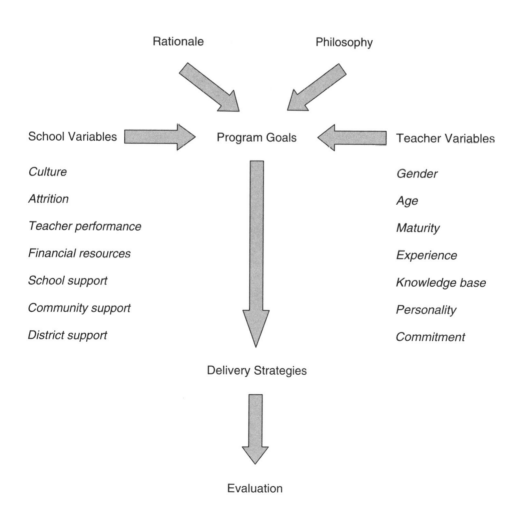

Rationale   Philosophy

School Variables → Program Goals ← Teacher Variables

Culture   *Gender*

Attrition   *Age*

Teacher performance   *Maturity*

Financial resources   *Experience*

School support   *Knowledge base*

Community support   *Personality*

District support   *Commitment*

Delivery Strategies

Evaluation

Resource B: Resources for Additional Information

Brock, B. L., & Grady, M. L. (2001). *From first-year to first-rate: Principals guiding new teachers* (2nd ed.). Thousand Oaks, CA: Corwin Press. This is a guide for administrators in developing a teacher induction plan to help new teachers become first-rate educators.

Chatlain, G. (2002). *Teacher induction in Catholic schools.* Unpublished master's thesis, University of Saskatchewan, Saskatoon, Saskatchewan, Canada. This thesis is a report of the unique issues and problems that confront new teachers in Catholic schools.

The Council of Chief State School Officers (www.ccsso.org). This is a consortium of state education agencies and national education organizations dedicated to reform of professional development for teachers.

Glickman, C. D., Gordon, S. P., & Ross-Gordon, J. M. (2004). *Supervision and instructional leadership: A developmental approach* (6th ed.). Needham Heights, MA: Allyn & Bacon. This is a classic text for assisting teachers in refining their teaching skills.

Gordon, S. P., & Maxey, S. (2000). *How to help new teachers succeed* (2nd ed.). Alexandria, VA: Association for Supervision and Curriculum Development. The authors present ideas and options to use in tailoring a beginning teacher assistance program.

Jones, F. (2001). *Fred Jones' tools for teachers.* Santa Cruz, CA: Fredric Jones & Associates. This book offers practical strategies on classroom instruction and management.

Jonson, K. F. (2002). *Being an effective mentor.* Thousand Oaks, CA: Corwin Press. Jonson's book offers practical ideas and concrete examples for mentors of new teachers.

National Board for Professional Teaching Standards (NBPTS; www.nbpts.org). This is an organization dedicated to effective teaching and improved student learning.

Oliva, P. F., & Pawlas, G. E. (2004). *Supervision for today's schools* (7th ed.). Hoboken, NJ: Wiley/Jossey-Bass. Chapter 5 of this book provides guidance for principals on assisting teachers with classroom management.

Portner, H. (2001). *Training mentors is not enough.* Thousand Oaks, CA: Corwin Press. This is a how-to guide and workbook for planning a mentoring program.

Portner, H. (2002). *Being mentored: A guide for protégés.* Thousand Oaks, CA: Corwin Press. This text is designed as a guide for the individual being mentored, the protégé.

Richin, R., Banyon, R., Stein, R. P., & Banyon, F. (2003). *Induction: Connecting teacher recruitment to retention.* Thousand Oaks, CA: Corwin Press. This book presents a framework for recruiting, developing, and retaining effective teachers.

Sweeny, B. W. (2001). *Leading the teacher induction and mentoring program.* Arlington Heights, IL: SkyLight Professional Development. The author provides guidance in developing and refining a mentoring program and includes a chapter on the use of technology to support novices and mentoring.

Villani, S. (2002). *Mentoring programs for new teachers: Models of induction and support.* Thousand Oaks, CA: Corwin Press. This text offers practitioners examples of practical applications of mentoring programs in a variety of settings.

References

Ashby, D. E., & Krug, S. E. (1998). *Thinking through the principalship.* Larchmont, NY: Eye on Education.

Barth, R. S. (1990). *Improving schools from within.* San Francisco: Jossey-Bass.

Bear, G. G. (2005). *Developing self-discipline and preventing and correcting behavior.* Needham Heights, MA: Pearson Allyn & Bacon.

Bolich, A. M. (2001). *Reduce your losses: Help new teachers become veteran teachers.* Atlanta, GA: Southern Regional Education Board. (ERIC Document Reproduction Service No. ED460121)

Brewster, C., & Railsback, J. (2001, May). *Supporting beginning teachers: How administrators, teachers, and policymakers can help new teachers succeed.* Portland, OR: Northwest Regional Educational Laboratory.

Brock, B. L. (1988). Profile of a beginning teacher. *Momentum, 21*(4), 54–57.

Brock, B. L., & Grady, M. L. (1998, January/February). Beginning teacher induction programs: The role of the principal. *Clearinghouse, 71*(3), 179–183.

Brock, B. L., & Grady, M. L. (2000). *Rekindling the flame: Principals combating teacher burnout.* Thousand Oaks, CA: Corwin Press.

Brock, B. L., & Grady, M. L. (2001). *From first-year to first-rate: Principals guiding new teachers* (2nd ed.).Thousand Oaks, CA: Corwin Press.

Burden, J. M., & Cooper, P. (2004). *An educator's guide to classroom management.* Boston: Houghton Mifflin.

Chatlain, G. (2002). *Teacher induction in Catholic schools.* Unpublished master's thesis, University of Saskatchewan, Saskatoon, Saskatchewan, Canada.

Cochran-Smith, M., & Lytle, S. (2001). Beyond certainty: Taking an inquiry stance on practice. In A. Liberman & L. Millers (Eds.), *Teachers caught in the action: Professional development that matters* (pp. 45–58). New York: Teachers College Press.

Cole, A. L. (1991, April 19–23). *Relationships in the workplace: Doing what comes naturally?* Paper presented at the annual meeting of the American Educational Research Association, Chicago.

Cole, A. L. (1993, April 12–16). *Problems and paradoxes in beginning teachers support: Issues concerning school administrators.* Paper presented at the annual meeting of the American Educational Research Association, Atlanta, GA.

Danielson, C. (1996). *Frameworks for teaching.* Alexandria, VA: Association for Supervision and Curriculum Development.

Darling-Hammond, L., & Sykes, G. (Eds.). (1999). *Teaching as the learning profession: Handbook of policy and practice.* San Francisco: Jossey-Bass.

Deal, T. E., & Peterson, K. D. (1990). *The principal's role in shaping school culture.* Washington, DC: Office of Educational Research and Improvement. (ERIC Document Reproduction Service No. ED325914)

DePaul, A. (2000). *Survival guide for new teachers: How new teachers can work effectively with veteran teachers, parents, principals, and teacher educators.* Washington, DC: Office of Educational Research and Improvement. Retrieved September 24, 2005, from http://www.ed.gov/teachers/become/about/survivalguide/survguide.pdf

Dexter, R., Berube, W., Moore, A., & Klopfenstein, M. (2005, February 17–20). *Key components of a new teacher induction and mentoring program.* Paper presented at the 137th annual meeting of the American Association of School Administrators National Conference, San Antonio, TX.

Dilworth, M. E., & Imig, D. G. (1995). Professional teacher development. *ERIC Review, 3*(3), 511.

Drago-Severson, E. (2004). *Helping teachers learn: Principal leadership for adult growth and development.* Thousand Oaks, CA: Corwin Press.

DuFour, R. (1999a). Challenging role. *Journal of Staff Development, 20*(4), 62–63.

DuFour, R. (1999b). Game plan. *Journal of Staff Development, 20*(2), 57–58.

Egan, B. L. (2002). *Administrative accountability and the novice teacher.* Paper presented at the annual meeting of the American Association of Colleges for Teacher Education, New York.

Feiman-Nemser, S., Carver, C., Schwille, S., & Yusko, B. (1999). Beyond support: Taking new teachers seriously as learners. In M. Scherer (Ed.), *A better beginning: Supporting and mentoring new teachers.* Alexandria, VA: Association for Supervision and Curriculum Development.

Fideler, E. F., & Haselkorn, D. (1999). *Learning the ropes.* Belmont, CA: Recruiting New Teachers.

Fullan, M. (2000). *Change forces: The sequel.* Philadelphia: George H. Buchanan.

Ganser, T. (2003). Sharing a cup of coffee is only the beginning. *Journal of Staff Development, 23*(4) 28–32.

Glasser, W. (1998). *Choice therapy in the classroom.* New York: HarperCollins.

Glickman, C. D., Gordon, S. P., & Ross-Gordon, J. M. (2004). *Supervision and instructional leadership: A developmental approach* (6th ed.). Needham Heights, MA: Allyn & Bacon.

Glickman, C. D., Gordon, S. P., & Ross-Gordon, J. M. (2005). *The basic guide to supervision and instructional supervision.* Needham Heights, MA: Allyn & Bacon.

Gordon, S. P. (2004). *Professional development for school improvement: Empowering learning communities.* Needham Heights, MA: Allyn & Bacon.

Grady, M. L. (in press). The status of children and families in the U.S. In *Encyclopedia of education leadership and administration.* Thousand Oaks, CA: Sage.

Hart, A., & Bredeson, P. (1996). *The principalship: A theory of professional learning and practice.* New York: McGraw-Hill.

Hodgkinson, H. L. (2002, November/December). Dealing with diversity. *Principal, 82*(2), 14. Retrieved July 22, 2005, from http://www.naesp.org

Ingersol, R. M., & Smith, T. M. (2003, May). The wrong solution to the teacher shortage. *Educational Leadership, 60*(8), 30–33.

Interstate New Teacher Assessment and Support Consortium (INTASC). (1996). *INTASC fact sheet.* Washington, DC: Council of Chief State School Officers.

Johnson, L., Freedman, S., Aschheim, B., & Krupp, V. L. (Eds.). (2003). *Mentoring works: A sourcebook for school leaders.* Newton, MA: Beginning Teacher Center of *Teachers 21* and Simmons College.

Jones, F. (2001). *Fred Jones' tools for teachers.* Santa Cruz, CA: Fredric H. Jones & Associates.

Jones, V. F., & Jones, L. S. (1998). *Comprehensive classroom management* (5th ed.). Needham Heights, MA: Allyn & Bacon.

Jonson, K. F. (2002). *Being an effective mentor: How to help beginning teachers succeed.* Thousand Oaks, CA: Corwin Press.

Kajs, L. T., Alaniz, R., Willman, E., Maier, J. N., Brott, P. E., & Gomez, D. M. (2003). Looking at the process of mentoring for beginning teachers. In L. Johnson, S. Freedman, B. Aschheim, & V. L. Krupp (Eds.), *Mentoring works: A sourcebook for school leaders* (pp. 63–69). Newton, MA: Beginning Teacher Center of *Teachers 21* and Simmons College.

Kauffman, J. M., Mostert, M. P., Trent, S. T., & Hallahan, D. P. (2002). *Managing classroom behavior: A reflective case-based approach* (3rd ed.). Needham Heights, MA: Allyn & Bacon.

Knowles, M. S. (1980). *The modern practice of adult education: From pedagogy to andragogy* (2nd ed.). Chicago: Association Press.

Larrivee, B. (2005). *Authentic classroom management: Creating a learning community and building reflective practice* (2nd ed.). Needham Heights, MA: Allyn & Bacon.

Leithwood, K. (1990). The principal's role in teacher development. In V. Joyce (Ed.), *Changing school culture through staff development* (pp. 71–90). Alexandria, VA: Association for Supervision and Curriculum Development.

Lenhardt, B. (2000). *The preparation and professional development of teachers in the Northwest: A depiction study.* Portland, OR: Northwest Regional Educational Laboratory.

Levin, J., & Nolan, J. F. (2004). *Principles of classroom management.* Needham Heights, MA: Pearson Allyn & Bacon.

Little, J. W. (1982). Norms of collegiality and experimentation: Workplace conditions of school success. *American Educational Research Journal, 19*(3), 325–340.

Moir, E. (2003, July 28–30). *Launching the next generation of teachers through quality induction.* Paper presented at the meeting of the National Commission on Teaching and America's Future, Denver, CO.

Northwest Regional Educational Laboratory (NWREL). (1997). *The need for diversifying the teacher workforce in the Northwest: Issues status, opportunities, and next steps.* Portland, OR: Author.

Oliva, P. F., & Pawlas, G. E. (2004). *Supervision for today's schools* (7th ed.). Hoboken, NJ: Wiley/Jossey-Bass.

Owens, R. G. (1995). *Organizational behavior in education* (5th ed.). Needham Heights, MA: Allyn & Bacon.

Pasch, S. H., Wolfe, M. P., Steffy, B. E., & Enz, B. J. (2000). Applying the life cycle. of the career teacher model. In B. J. Steffy, M. P. Wolfe, S. H. Pasch, & B. J. Enz (Eds.), *Life cycle of the career teacher* (pp. 104–118). Thousand Oaks, CA: Corwin Press.

Peterson, K. D. (1999, Spring). Time uses flows from school cultures: River of values and traditions can nurture or poison staff development hours. *Journal of Staff Development, 20*(2), 1–7.

Portner, H. (2001). *Training mentors is not enough.* Thousand Oaks, CA: Corwin Press.

Raywid, M. (1993, September). Finding time for collaboration. *Educational Leadership, 51,* 30–34.

Recruiting New Teachers (RNT). (2000). *A guide to developing teacher induction programs.* Belmont, MA: Author.

Runyan, C. K. (1991, November 22–26). *Empowering beginning teachers through developmental induction.* Paper presented at the 16th Annual National Conference of the National Council of States on Inservice Education, Houston, TX.

Sargent, B. (2003, May). Finding good teachers and keeping them. *Educational Leadership, 60*(8), 44–47.

Sergiovanni, T. J. (2006). *The principalship* (5th ed.). Boston: Allyn & Bacon.

Sergiovanni, T. J., & Starratt, R. J. (2002). *Supervision: A redefinition* (7th ed.). Boston: McGraw-Hill.

Steffy, B. E., Wolfe, M. P., Pasch, S. H., & Enz, B. J. (2000). *Life cycle of the career teacher.* Thousand Oaks, CA: Corwin Press.

Wayson, W. W., DeVoss, G. G., Kaeser, S. C., Lasley, T., Pinnell, S. S., & Phi Delta Kappa Commission on Discipline. (1982). *Handbook for developing schools with good discipline.* Bloomington, IN: Phi Delta Kappa.

Zepeda, S. J. (1999). *Staff development: Practices that promote leadership in learning communities.* Larchmont, NJ: Eye on Education.

Index

**CORWIN
PRESS**

The Corwin Press logo—a raven striding across an open book—represents
the union of courage and learning. Corwin Press is committed to improving
education for all learners by publishing books and other professional
development resources for those serving the field of PreK–12 education. By
providing practical, hands-on materials, Corwin Press continues to carry
out the promise of its motto: **"Helping Educators Do Their Work Better."**